Hired!

Wishing you all the best!
Ty. ☺

You got this always!
-Hibo ♡

Hired!

How To Get The Zippy Gig.

Insider Secrets From A Top Recruiter.

2nd Edition.

Sheila Musgrove

I would like to graciously acknowledge all of the people I've quoted for their cleverly written words. I've made every effort to determine if their quotes were included in previously published material and required permission to reprint. If I've printed in error, please accept my apologies. Corrections will be made in future editions.

Book cover & interior formatting: Goran Tovilovic, www.bookclaw.com
Book front & back cover author photo: Kirstey Jane, www.supercorporatepeople.com
Illustrations: Bro Ojrot – Instagram: @broojrot
Makeup: Allyson Vandervaate – Instagram: @ssavagemakeup

Join me in the conversation about "Hired!":
Instagram: @sheilamusgrove_author
Twitter: @SMusgrove_TAG
LinkedIn: https://www.linkedin.com/in/sheilamusgrove/
Enroll in my blog: www.sheilamusgrove.com

ISBN Hardcover: 978-1-9991041-3-9
ISBN Softcover: 978-1-9991041-2-2
ISBN E-book: 978-1-9991041-4-6

Dedication:

For My Mom & Dad: Betty & Gene Musgrove, with Love.

This dedication appeared in my first edition. "Hired!" will always be dedicated to you both.

I won the parent lottery with you two. I've had a lifetime of fabulousness from you both—where do I even start?

You taught me what a solid work ethic and truly *showing up* each day means. Thank you for giving me such a strong vision of what it takes to be a successful entrepreneur and create a successful business.

You taught me that B students could actually do whatever the hell they wanted for a career. You gave me my first speaking gig and helped me to write my first story in grade 4—perhaps that's where this all started?!

You've been my biggest fans with unwavering support and encouragement in whatever I've chosen to do. (OK, except for that brief dream of being a saxophone player in a rock band – you were right, it probably wasn't the best idea and thanks goodness is was a short-lived dream. SMILE.

I'm grateful for a really normal childhood. I know how hard you both worked in your careers to make it really fabulous. As I get older, it amazes me how you did it all.

Two memorable questions you asked me were:

Dad asked, *"Are you ever going to finish school and get a real job?"* Yes, a reasonable question after a clerk-typist certificate, legal assistant diploma and a degree. (And thank you for attending each one of my convocation ceremonies!)

Mom said to the 13-year-old me, *"You'd better get a really good job because you've got expensive taste and you really like clothes, shoes and jewelry."* Good advice, Mom!

Funny that both questions were about me *finding my fabulous Zippy Gig*!

I'm the luckiest girl in the world to have been blessed with your immense love and support.

Acknowledgements:

I'd like to thank some really special people:

Mom-Betty. Thank you for always being my biggest cheerleader.

Kim Duke, writer extraordinaire—who knew after meeting years ago that we'd be wrapping up our third book project! Years after publishing the first edition of "Hired!", I'm still grateful you helped me to find my fun, sassy writing voice. Thank goodness—it's a hell of a lot more fun than the fork-in-the-eye style I started with all those years ago! Thank you for the endless round of edits, encouragement and kicks in the a$$. GRIN. You're the best.

Bro Ojrot – my amazing illustrator. Seriously, you've nailed my hair. Your images have taken my last two books to a new level of fun and cool. They make my book and keynotes memorable. Thank you for the endless rounds of edits to get things "just right".

Goran Tovilovic – your formatting finesse ensured my book looked flawless.

Kirstey Jane – my talented photographer. I love our photoshoots – thank you for working your magic!

To all of the amazing candidates I've had the pleasure of working with at TAG Recruitment and those who've enlisted my trust for resume writing and interview coaching.

My fabulous team at TAG - We've proven that humour belongs in a workplace. Thank you for holding down the fort on the days I was working to get this project across the finish line and the days when I'm out presenting and travelling. What you do each day allows me the opportunity to do what I love most—delivering keynotes and writing. Thank you for all you do!

Thank you to all of the job seekers around the world who purchased a copy of the 1st edition of HIRED! I loved hearing your job search success stories!

Your Support of *Hired!* Also Helps Canadian Veterans.

When you purchase a copy of "Hired!", you're also helping Canadian veterans.

10% of the net proceeds of each book will be donated to various charities who support Canadian veterans.

I'm passionate about helping all job seekers, including veterans, to remove barriers to getting their resume noticed and building confidence about interviewing.

Thank you for your support!

Table Of Contents:

Prologue:

Welcome to the 2nd edition of ***Hired! How To Get The Zippy Gig. Insider Secrets From A Top Recruiter***. Your job search just became much easier!

When I launched ***Hired!*** to the world in 2016, I had nooooooooooo idea what would happen in the days, months and years afterward.

Within 24 hours, ***Hired!*** hit the Amazon best-seller ranks in both Canada and the USA. Within 6 days, it was in the #1 spot!

I've presented my ***Hired!*** keynote for thousands of job seekers throughout Canada, the USA and internationally. Job seekers around the world have told me that my book helped them land their new zippy gigs. And, that makes me very happy!

Job seekers from around the world, at all levels and professions, have used ***Hired!*** to demystify resume writing and interviewing.

I want to give hope to people who suddenly find themselves out of work or who want to switch to a new career and the media has helped me spread the word! I regularly appear on a number of Canadian television shows: CTV at Noon, Breakfast Television Morning, Global Morning, CHCH and radio including CBC, 660 & 770 news radio.

Now, more than ever, people need help on how to find a job.

The pandemic has affected most of us.
And if you've lost your job or
you've decided to switch careers?
***Hired!* helps you every step of the way.**

I remember thinking on New Years' Eve 2019, that 2020 had a magical ring to it! Like most of us, I had all sorts of grand plans for the year. We had no idea what lurked around the corner.

I remember the days leading up to the pandemic.

Sure, we heard of this little virus circulating on the other side of the world. I thought, *Gosh, it's never going to land over here in Canada*. So, I was off doing my thing. I had an interview on CTV a few days before the pandemic was officially announced. I did a book signing that same afternoon at a local Indigo/Chapters and then a follow up signing at another store the next day. ***All was normal, right?*** And, then the state of emergency was called. GULP.

Who knew in the next few days, the world of work and life in general was going to change, ***forever***?

I said to my team, "Oh this work from home bit...it's going to be a couple of weeks, max. And, then we'll be back to the office." Wow, was I wrong. In the weeks that followed, I was freaked out. ***And, I'm not a "freak out" kind of gal.***

Like you, I was concerned about my livelihood. *Was my business going to make it? If everyone is sick and can't go to work, my temporary staffing firm was certainly going to be on shaky ground.* It was a scary time. People were losing their jobs at a crazy pace.

"In Canada, over 3 million people lost their job as a result of the pandemic."

Source: Bloomberg

And, they were worried about how and where the heck they were going to find a job in the middle of the pandemic. My phone rang off the hook with people looking for help and for jobs.

An epiphany hit. I was going to do something to help job seekers.

I took my *Hired!* presentation and chopped it into a 3-part series of 20-minute webinars. *(When people are freaked out, their attention span is short.)*

I normally charge for doing my presentations. But this wasn't the time to be charging job seekers. So, I launched a FREE webinar series for them. I thought it would be a 1-round series of the 3 webinars. *(And silly me, I thought the pandemic would be done by then too! HA)*. Well, every last seat was scooped up in the first round. And, the pandemic continued. So, I offered it again. And, again.

26 free webinars later I had over 1000 job seekers, at all career levels from <u>around the globe</u> attend my 3-part series.

It felt really good to help and share my knowledge. Searching for a job, writing resumes and interviewing is, at the best of times, stressful, but layer in a pandemic and the stress level was off the damn charts.

As you'll soon see by reading this book - I'm a recruiter with a sense of humour. Did we ever need a laugh or two during those early weeks and months of the pandemic. I gave hope to 1000+ job seekers that writing a resume and interviewing was going to be fun and easy.
And, that's what I do for you in the pages of this book – demystify how to write a resume and how to love interviewing! **Yes, love**.

Much has changed in the job search process since the pandemic. Video interviews are used extensively, which were rare pre-pandemic. I've written an entire chapter dedicated to "Acing the Video Interview." Throughout the lockdowns, we all had to work from home – balancing home schooling, child care, pets, spouses and the new world of work. There's a chapter on remote work as well.

Let's face it. The pre-pandemic world isn't coming back. How we search for jobs and work in our careers is forever different.

Let's embrace it.

Yes, that was me giving you a big virtual hug.

Introduction:

Are you ready to learn how to get HIRED and get the Zippy Gig?

The burning question you're probably thinking – *What the hell is a Zippy Gig?*

The word zippy is used frequently in my office. Who doesn't smile when saying the word ZIPPY?

Zippy Gigs are part of my fun, silly language. Why use dull words when you can have sparkly ones? (Being a little weird has definitely helped me create one of the hottest recruitment firms in Canada.)

When you give your job search a fun name like zippy, your dreaded job search turns into an exciting adventure.

When my team does business development research – which as we all know – is a little dull, it's way more fun to say,

I'm working on finding new Zippy Gigs.

So, the name just seemed to be a natural fit for the book.

Who wouldn't want a job described as a ZIPPY GIG?

The idea of writing a resume and going on interviews might feel daunting. Rest assured, I will make the process of being HIRED and getting the Zippy Gig beyond fun for you.

Let's get the Zippy started.

You've searched the business aisle of the book store for fast job-hunting advice. (And you've seen how cheesy and DULL most career books are!)

Well, GREAT news.

This isn't your average, boring, mind-numbing, HR type of book on resumes and interviews.

Get ready to DITCH EVERYTHING you've ever learned about writing a resume and toss it out the window.

You'll learn step by step how to write a kick-ass resume that gets your phone ringing for interviews for your Zippy Gig

I'll Show You My Insider Secrets.

And just how do I know the Insider Secrets and what you need to get hired?

I've been in Agency Recruitment for close to 20 years. I launched my firm TAG Recruitment Group in 2005. I've decoded what makes a resume kick-ass and shiny to employers and what makes a winning interview. My company, TAG Recruitment, has won national awards and been recognized by Profit & Alberta Venture Magazines as a top growth company and me as one of Canada's top 100 women entrepreneurs.

As I did more candidate interviews, it was obvious that most people were lost in the dark when it came to resumes and interviews. I mean LOST.

I shared my formula for kick-ass shiny resumes for my candidates and then...

THE MAGIC STARTED HAPPENING.

The results were immediate.

My candidates were more confident with their finished resume and excited to deliver an out-of-the-park interview. Thousands of candidates have taken my one-on-one coaching to secure their Zippy Gig.

I'm super excited to take the lessons learned from those interviews and break it down into an easy-to-use format for you. It's called the 2-step resume formula.

And you'll have a laugh or two!

The best part?

You'll have a shiny resume that gets your phone ringing with opportunity.

Let's get to work and get YOU into a fabulous new ZIPPY GIG.

You'll create a shiny kick-ass resume AND, you'll be uber-prepared to deliver an off the charts, rockstar type of interview.

You'll be the interviewee they drool over.

You'll walk into ANY interview exuding confidence.

The idea of bringing your 2-3 resume pages to life will have you bursting with excitement.

Yes, sunshine, bursting.

You'll be beyond prepared and you'll have the insight of knowing what a hiring manager wants to hear in an interview.

Imagine walking out of your next interview on Cloud 9, knowing you aced the interview. *(Yes, that will be you.)*

This book contains not only how to write a shiny kick-ass resume and how to rock an interview. I show you all the nuts and bolts in between. I also share the downright silly things that can send a star candidate resume straight to the recycle bin.

"The secret to getting started is getting started."

Mark Twain

CHAPTER 1
Let's Get The Zippy Started

There are loads of reasons why you're looking for a new *Zippy Gig*.

Do You Fit One of These 8 Scenarios?

1. You've Been Laid Off:

If you've been through a layoff – you probably feel terrified of being without work and an income.

The uncertainty of how long it will take to find a new role is unsettling and unnerving for sure.

And, the last thing you want is fear seeping through in an interview! (And, believe me, hiring managers and recruiters can sense fear.)

I've got a full juicy chapter on how to handle lay-offs and another on handling gaps in your resume. Was that a big sigh of relief I heard?

2. You're Not Growing. And You're Bored To Death In Your Job:

Are you in a situation where you're simply **bored to tears** in your current role? You've tackled every challenge in the role and you're ready for new challenges.

You're tired of being paid to watch paint dry.

That's what it feels like when you aren't being challenged. Or maybe you just don't have enough to do.

You want to be on the edge of your seat and feel excited about going to work again!

3. You Want To Do A Career Pivot:

You're ready for a 180-degree spin into something new and exciting. I've got a full chapter just for you!

Have you been doing the same job for years? You went to school for it, or maybe because it was expected you'd join the family business.

You know in your heart you want to take the leap into a profession you've always dreamed of.

4. Your Job Just Isn't The Right Fit:

Are you in a situation where your work environment, day-to-day job duties, boss or colleagues don't align with what makes you happy?

Perhaps your ideas are being squashed, or creativity isn't encouraged – *maybe the carpet smells* – it doesn't matter.

Something just doesn't feel right for you and you're ready to exit stage left.

I interviewed a candidate who chose to leave her company as her boss would actually throw things. Seriously! She drew the line at a laptop being tossed her way.

Yes, we're happy to report, she's now with a nice organization with a firm "no throwing" policy! The only things they throw at her are compliments.

5. You've Been Let Go:

Oh dear. That's a tough one. I've dedicated an entire chapter to dealing with the *BIG T*. If this is you, zip over to *Chapter 7, The Big T – Terminations & Other Tough Conversations*. Trust me, once you read it, you'll feel better!

6. You're Going Back to Work OR Starting Your Career:

After taking time off, you've decided it's time to go back to work. You might be a little nervous about how to cover time off for family commitments or maybe you've been travelling the world. I've got a chapter on how to cover gaps in your resume. You haven't been sitting idle. You'll love the creative ideas in the Gap chapter.

7. You're fresh out of College or University:

Congratulations! You're looking for your first exciting new gig. I share many ways to make your skills, education and background a stand out. Trust me, you'll grin ear to ear and exude confidence with your new shiny resume.

8. You LOVE Working From Home:

You've made the big adjustment to remote work and you've grown to LOVE it. But your employer has made it clear they'd love everyone back in the office, as soon as it's safe to do so. You're not happy about it. So, you've decided to look for a new gig with the flexibility for remote work. I've got a full chapter on remote work just for you!

We'll walk through how to find your new **Zippy Gig** together.

And, once you know what the heck to put on a resume and how to get through an interview with confidence and ease, you'll GRIN ear to ear!

Candidates I've worked with practically skip out of my office like they've been handed a secret code. *(And they have been.)* They also have a wee bit of disbelief on how easy it all is.

That'll be you too!!

Let's get the Zippy started!

"There are no shortcuts to any place worth going."

Beverley Sills

CHAPTER 2

Send Your Rusty Resume to the Recycle Bin

I've read thousands of resumes and I think thousands of people have read the same bad advice. Why?

Everyone creates the same dull resume. WE need to find that boring resume book and bury it. (Or, maybe we should keep the secrets to writing shiny resumes just between us.)

I'm going to be BOLD here.

BORING RESUMES DON'T GET RESULTS.

I call BORING resumes RUSTY. Yes, they're old and rusty.

RUSTY defined: "Faded or shabby; impaired by time" (Source: Dictionary.com)

If your resume is boring *(and impaired by time)* your phone won't ring.

It's as simple as that.

Here's a FACT that will shock you...

"80% of resumes are rejected in less than 11 seconds."

Peter Harris, Financial Post

Your resume at first viewing gets 11 SECONDS max by a hiring manager or recruiter.

Yes, that's it.

Let me ask you – *what percentile does your resume fall in?*

Are you in the *80% being sent to the recycle bin*? Or the *elite 20%* who make it through the first cut in those precious 11 seconds?

If I was a betting woman, I'd guess you're in the *DREADED 80% pile.*

Here's the *GREAT* news.

You'll learn my Insider SECRETS so YOU *will be* in the elite 20% in those first 11 seconds.

Want to know how resumes are actually read?

Remember the last trashy or sci-fi novel you read? You devoured every delectable word. Eagerly flipping pages, and not missing a **single** detail in the fabulous story.

You might think your resume gets read EXACTLY that same way.

Word by word by word.

WRONG. Not a chance.

Everyone thinks that's how they're read, *so you're in good company.*

Employers & Recruiters Read Your Resume Like *A* Magazine

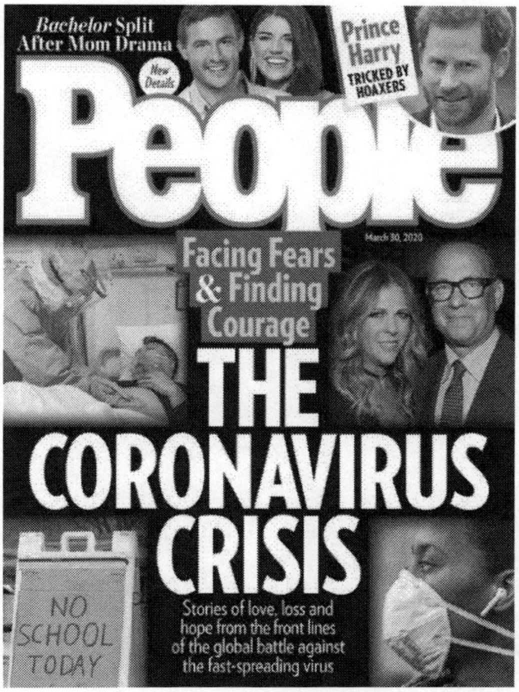

Resumes are read like how you scan a magazine while waiting in the grocery store checkout line.

You quickly flip through the pages to find the article that caught your attention. You're after the juicy stuff. That's it.

You SKIM.

That's really how employers and recruiters read resumes too.

We skim for the JUICY stuff.

Who has time to read an entire magazine?

Two minutes brings us up to date on the comings and goings of all our favourite celebrities.

Your resume is exactly like a magazine.

You only get 11 SECONDS to highlight the "comings and goings" of your career.

When you skim through a magazine at the grocery store, you decide quickly if you're buying this magazine or moving onto another.

After 11 seconds of skimming your resume, I decide if I'm buying your pitch. (And, by "buying", I mean picking up the phone to have a conversation with you.)

6 Surprising Things that Get <u>ZERO Attention</u> in the 11 Second First Cut.

1. Career Summary & Highlights:

Yes, it's true. I know you've poured over thesaurus.com to pick the most eloquent, juicy, buzzy words to describe how *AMAZING* you are. (I'm sure you're amazing, we just need to show your AMAZINGNESS in other CLEVER ways.)

Why? 11 seconds.

Assume that everything on the top part of your resume doesn't get read. And, even if there are numbers, they'll likely get missed.

2. Target Position*:*

Target position rarely gets read…because <u>it's not targeted</u>. GRIN. It's usually something like this…

I'm looking for a rewarding and demanding career with an organization with a strong corporate social presence, with career growth opportunities.

I have no idea if you want to be the receptionist or the payroll manager.

Target position needs to be targeted. More specifically, if you have a target position on your resume it needs to be the EXACT title of the role you're applying for.

3. ALL of those mind-numbing bullets:

The long list of bullet points listed under each role that describe what your functional responsibilities were in each job. *Nope, not reading those*. (Stay with me. I'll show you how to replace those bullets with impactful, concise detail that WILL get read.) Sure, I absolutely want to know what each of your jobs were, but there's a far better way than the mind-numbing bullets!

5. Interests:

Interests rarely get read because they're boringgggggggggggg.

Skiing, snowboarding, wine tasting, craft beer, cooking...sure these are all really fun things to do, but they look exactly like the last 47 resumes I've read.

The exception is if you've written something **INTERESTING**.

One way to be interesting is to be unusual. One of the recruiters I hired wrote that one of his interests was Dodgeball. That little quirk made me laugh and I picked up the phone to call him.

Why? Because it was something I'd never seen on a resume. And, well, who doesn't smile when remembering Dodgeball from grade school?

Have you jumped out of a plane? Travelled? Grown award-winning tomatoes? What do you do for fun?

Don't be afraid to stand out and show a bit of personality.

You just never know what cool conversation will spark based on your fun interests.

The 11 Second Skim:

You're likely scratching your head wondering what the heck gets read in those quick 11 seconds? Hiring managers and recruiters are professional skimmers. We're great speed readers. Based on the sheer volume of resumes received, we can only SKIM.

The 5 Things That <u>ARE</u> SKIMMED:

Skim #1: Your current and last positions: Company name and your job titles only. Job titles tell us quickly what kind of role and level you've been working at previously. In a nano-second it tells us if previous roles would align to the role we're looking to fill.

Skim #2: Start and end dates (HINT: we look for GAPS in dates – you might have run off to the circus or been unemployed – either way, we want to know. More on this later.)

Ideally when one position stops, another starts immediately after. But, hey, life happens and gaps in your employment happen. I cover some clever ways to cover gaps in Chapter 6: *How To Do A Career Pivot...Without Getting Dizzy.*

Skim #3: Education*:* If I'm looking for a specific educational background, the skim may start and stop with education. If you've got the education I'm looking for, I'll continue on with the skim. If you don't, well, the skim stops there.

Skim #4: Location. *A quick glance back up to the top to check* where you're located. Are we in the same city or country?

Skim #5: *Numbers & percentages* *always get a quick glance if they're in the body of the resume.* More on #'s and %'s in a bit. (Kudos to you if you have results on your resume already! Don't fret if you don't. You'll have piles of numbers on your resume by the time you're done this book!)

There you go. That's what 11 seconds gets you.

Tick...Tick...Tick...

11 Seconds zips by in a flash!

The New Rules of Resumes:

RUSTY is out.

SHINY is in.

Don't settle for a rusty resume. There isn't a second to waste in keeping that old rusty thing.

You have a fleeting 11 seconds to grab an employer's attention. But a rusty resume is a fast track to their recycle bin.

No call.
No interview.
No job.

Shiny catches their eye.

But don't fret. It's easy to shine your resume up.

Because a shiny resume is all about YOUR RESULTS.

It's time to show off the cool, amazing, impressive things you've done! (And I'll show you how to find them ESPECIALLY when you don't think you have them.)

However, before we move into SHINY, let's see if your resume passes the rusty test.

They might even need sunglasses it will be so darn bright!

In my keynotes, I love sharing this rusty car to drive home my point about rusty resumes. I think we can agree this is a car. But if you need this rusty car to get you to a destination...*you're not moving an inch.*

Your resume is the same. The one saved in your computer IS NOT the one you need. And, like this rusty car, *it's not going to get you anywhere with your job search.*

When I speak about rusty resumes, most audience attendees look down, avoid eye contact with me because secretly they're thinking, *She's soooooo wrong, my resume is NOT rusty.*

Maybe that thought just crossed your mind too.

Hmmmm. Let's put your resume through my filter.

4 Signs You Own A Rusty Resume:

- You've sent out hundreds of resumes and you're not getting any calls.
- You have no idea why you're not getting calls because your experience is EXACTLY what they are asking for.
- You follow up on your applications, but no one returns your calls.
- Zero job action. Period.

The Verdict: Your resume IS RUSTY.

Guess what hiring managers and recruiters see in resume after resume?

A long list of MIND-NUMBING bullets that describe your functional responsibilities.

I call them BORING, OLD-SCHOOL RESUMES. They don't work.

Here's A Chunk Of A Boring, RUSTY Resume: ***Don't Do This At Home***.

ABC Company, Account Executive **2020 – Present**

- Responsible for cold calling.
- Did networking and marketing as required.
- Sold many new accounts in the Calgary area.
- Wrote proposals and met with clients.
- Handled objections.

The old-style resume is a real job killer and the fastest way to hit the 80% REJECT pile.

Why?

You're back to a BORING list of bullets that describe what you were responsible for in each role.

Do I actually read those bullets?

Not a chance.

Because there's RARELY anything worth reading.

We just skip them.

This worn-out old formula makes your resume look like every other resume out there.

(Even worse is when you use Times New Roman font. 99.9% of resumes use it.)

OK, are you with me here? Rusty doesn't work.

The worst part about a rusty resume? I have nooooooooo idea if you're the top performer on the team or if you're a day away from getting a pink slip. Rusty resumes only tell me what your jobs have been. That's just boring. And, it's not going to do anything to get you noticed.

But here's the GREAT news – you're going to learn how your resume can be a knock out in 11 seconds!

The secrets are in Chapter 4 and the big magic is in Chapter 5. I know you're excited but dive into Chapter 4 first!

CHAPTER 3
The Bones of Your Super Shiny Resume

Let's ease into this task of creating your shiny resume.

Getting started can feel overwhelming. Believe me, I get it.

Which is why we'll focus on the bones of your resume, first.

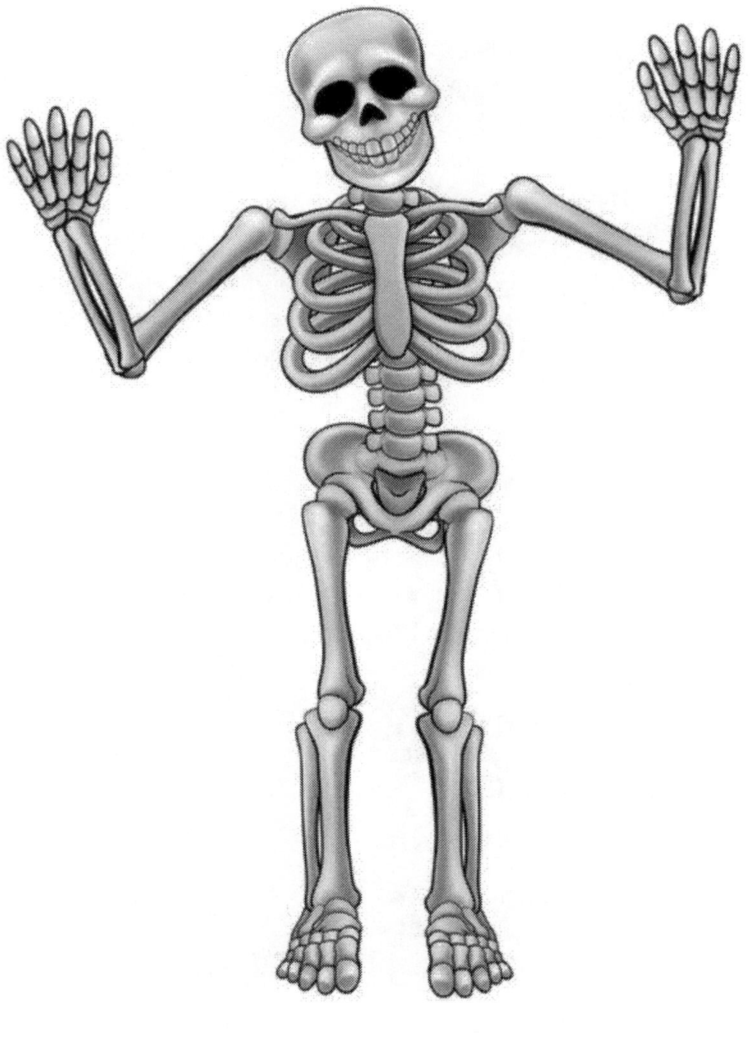

What are the bones?

They are the big picture - the structure.

Just like a house, if your resume doesn't have a solid foundation, it will likely cause problems, and we don't want that to happen.

Because we want this shiny resume to do some heavy lifting for you!

5 Shiny Resume Bones To Get You Started:

Let's look at the bones of a shiny resume. Good bones give your shiny new resume a solid and professional structure.

1. RESUME LENGTH: How many pages?

If you're fresh out of high school or college, one page is fine. Once you have a few years of experience, you should aim for a maximum of three pages.

Experienced professionals with at least three years' experience should always be longer than one page. If it's only one page, you've likely missed adding your successes. We'll talk about the importance of outlining successes – "the magic" in the next chapter.

And, as a recruiter, I'd be dashing back to my printer looking for the rest of your resume. (Yes – I can really dash in stilettos!)

But I don't you want you to go THIS FAR:

One of my resume coaching clients was a super smart, incredibly accomplished, global executive. His career spanned a few decades, multiple countries and mind boggling off-the-charts projects. When we met, his resume was a staggering 14 pages.

Yes, 14 pages of mind-numbing bullets! GASP.

I wasn't sure I was even going to take on the massive project of working with him. Well, I did. We applied the same 2-step resume formula you'll read about in Chapter 4 and we distilled his resume down to three powerfully succinct pages.

His complicated, drawn-out resume was now easy to understand and his skills were easy to see. And, because it was no longer a War and Peace novel, his phone rang off the hook for interviews! Yours will too!

2. CHRONOLOGICAL: And, how far back?

Your resume should always be reverse *chronological*. That means your most recent job is listed first and then you go backward. (<u>Never the opposite</u>.) If the first job on your resume starts 10 years ago, it looks like you haven't worked in a really long time. So, I'll stop reading and send your resume straight to the recycle bin. You don't want that.

Grouping roles by skill or job type is like trying to read a short story in a bowl of alphabet soup. (I loved Alphagetti as a kid!)

The Rule of 10:

Don't go back to the beginning of time in your resume.

Go back 10 years or to high school.

Don't go back to elementary school. GRIN. I don't need to know how you excelled at finger painting.

You can go back further if a role falls in the middle of that 10-year mark. I certainly don't recommend going back further than 15 years.

And, if you think about it, your skills and experience from the last 10 years is more in line with the type of job you seek now, versus the type of role you did 15 or 20 years ago.

I love the 80's: - The crazy hair styles. The ridiculous fashions. The cool music.

But that was a longgggggg time ago. And, frankly so were the 90's and 2000's. I coach candidates to take off any reference to a date from the 2000's or earlier. Why? Well, my recruiters were born somewhere in the 90's – 2000's. You'll remind them of their mom or dad. And, Mom or Dad might not be right for the gig.

3. What FONT SIZES Should You Use?

Your name: 14 – 16 – max 20 (bold)

Resume categories: 12 – 14 (bold)

Company name & Titles: 12 (bold)

Resume content: 10 – 11

Different font sizes and bolding help the reader to visually understand your resume sections. When we skim, the font sizes help the hiring manager to absorb more information faster.

Anything over a 20 font is just YELLING.

A 9 font or smaller is *WHISPERING*.

4. MARGINS: Microsoft Word has pre-set margins. Leave them alone. They're perfect for a great resume layout.

And don't even think of stretching the margins!

I know you're trying to be a great resume writing student. You're on a roll, following all my advice – you're grinning from ear to ear because your resume looks amazing!

You're just about done, but a few lines overflowed to a 4th page. Ugh.

You remember the maximum 3-page rule.

You think – *She'll never notice if I stretch those margins out, just a wee bit.*

So, you stretch the top and bottom margins. Darn. You still need to get a few words off that 4th page. You then pull out the left and right margins. The margins are stretched out so far, the words are dripping off the edges of the page.

DON'T DO IT!

When a hiring manager is doing the 11-second skim, white space is needed for them to take in more content.

Without white space, it's really difficult to read.

When you've crammed each page, it actually works against you.

So, guess what? Now your resume **received LESS than 11 seconds.**

Leave the damn margins alone. GRIN.

5. FORMATTING: How To Avoid Sending Your Resume Into The Black Hole

If you're uploading to a resume capture system, (called an ATS or an Applicant Tracking System) a few things will make it **disappear into thin air** before it is even read.

You really don't want that.

3 Silly Formatting Errors To Avoid:

1. Putting your contact details into a text box – what can happen is that it simply tells the system there's absolutely nothing to see! And, voila, you're lost forever.

2. Filling your resume with text boxes for the content or various sections – it ends up looking like alphabet soup more often than not.

3. PDF files often don't convert well. So, a good Word.doc is the best route.

Job seekers often GASP at this point. I always hear, "Someone could change my resume if I use a Word doc!" Believe me, recruiters and hiring managers are too damn busy to think about changing your resume. And, why on earth would anyone want to? Use a Word doc and you'll be golden.

Additional Formatting Recommendations:

- Don't add borders around your resume or heavy formatting. Start with a blank Word document and we'll build from there.

- When you're using a header, use the actual header for formatting. If you guess where the header should fall on the second page...well, you've just told the recruiter you could use a brush up on Word as you don't know how to insert a header. (Yikes!)

- Photos of your gorgeous face shouldn't appear. However, an exception is if you're in an industry where your look is part of the position. One example I recently encountered was for an interior design role. Her look was part of her brand and how she marketed her services. It worked.

- Select a font other than Times New Roman! It was the default font FOREVER and it makes your resume look like the last 4000 resumes I've read. Stand out with Calibri, Tahoma or Arial.

- Never use the comic font for your resume. Yes, we have seen it many times. We're not looking for a super hero. And, while we're at it. Avoid using script font or italics. It looks like you're inviting me to a tea party.

YOUR CONTACT DETAILS: Let's Start At The Top

Your name. Use the name you wish to be called. If your name is Robert, but you answer to Bob, use Bob. Use the name you answer to on daily basis.

Speaking of names...if you have a difficult to pronounce name, consider a phonetic spelling.

I worked with an amazing candidate named Guillermo. When I called, I immediately asked, "How do I properly pronounce your name?"

He replied with this phrasing, "Gee – Ar – Mo". EASY! We put the phonetic spelling in brackets on the top of his resume to help future hiring managers pronounce his name correctly.

Your formal legal name is only required on your payroll forms. There's no need to use your middle name on your resume – just a first and last name.

Don't include your home address on your resume. It can be left off for confidentiality reasons. Simply list the city and province you're located in. If all of your roles have been in the same city, you actually don't have to put the city.

If you're relocating, you can put a note at the top of your resume, below your contact details that reads:

Relocating to (city) upon securing employment.

(And, this is when a small font is OK.)

If you're relocating to a different country OR if you're attending school in a new country and you wish to pursue your career there, talk about your work eligibility at the top of your resume as well.

Permanent Residency application is pending approval.

Student Visa valid until 20XX.

Help a future employer to know what their investment in your employability status would need to be if you were hired.

One last tip if you're relocating – add the city to your target position. It just reaffirms your intention to move.

Target Position: Account Manager in (city).

You absolutely need a phone number – ideally just your cell. (Oh, and you don't have to write the words cell and email before writing them...we know what an email and phone number look like.) GRIN.

Your email address should be your first and last name and should display as such. Job searching is the time to amp up your professionalism.

Cute email addresses such as cutiepie16@hotmail.com or golfguy92@yahoo.ca should never be used on a resume. Similarly, your year of birth shouldn't be used as you're just telling the world how old you are. And, no need to spill those beans.

Here's a quick test.

Imagine the hiring manager from your dream company calls you to say they're sending a job offer and they ask you to confirm your email address...*did you just cringe?* Yeah, change it to your name.

And, while we're on email addresses...

Avoid made up words: ingadangadonkachit@.... Or Illi_chillin@

Your email address isn't always clickable for a hiring manager, keep in mind if your email address has to be retyped or shared over the phone – what are the odds a spelling mistake could happen? With the above two email addresses, I'd say the odds are pretty darn good!

Use your name and have your email display as your name. I worked with a candidate called Vern. He chose to have his email display as V. That's it. And, it hit my spam folder every single time.

The more times a hiring manager sees your name...the BETTER!

OK, this one might top the list for dumb ways to have your email address appear: **Me.** Don't do that.

Ditch the silly email addresses. You'll thank me for it.

Here's An Example:

Kris Smith

403-555-1234 kris.smith@gmail.com

(Pssst. You don't have to put the words "cell" or "email" in front of each—everyone knows what a phone number and email look like. GRIN.)

10 Shiny Resume Categories: Get Your 11 Seconds Of Sparkle!

An Important & Sassy Sheila Note: I'll cover 10 shiny categories, however, not all 10 get attention in 11 seconds. Some sections as we've talked about - might ***never even get read***, **EVER**.

And, don't use all 10 categories—use only the ones that showcase your background the best.

Let's start with 2 that almost <u>*NEVER*</u> get read:

1. **Career Summary or Highlights:** Can be included, but ***assume it won't be read.***

If you use a career summary and you've noted important highlights or awards, be sure to put them in the body of your resume under the role when they were achieved.

The first page of your resume is critical. In those 11 seconds, I might not get to page 2 of your career summary, so you need to make page 1 count. If you do a Career Summary section, DO NOT use a third of the first page. **You want as much of your career history as possible on the first page.**

You get it. I'm not a fan of a Career Summary section. If you do include, keep it BRIEF!

2. **Target Position:** We've already talked about silly vague target positions. Don't do that.

Pssst. **The target position should be the exact title of the role you're applying for**. GRIN.

If you're apply for multiple positions, you want to customize for each role. **Be specific.**

LESS is more:

Experienced Administrative professional, seeking an Executive Assistant role.

Strong hunter seeking a Senior New Business Development position.

Experienced Forklift Operator seeking a day shift position.

University graduate seeking an entry level Sales position.

The 2 most Important Sections Are: Career History & Education.

That's where most of the 11 seconds is focused.

Giving attention to these 2 key shiny areas ensures your 11 seconds count.

1. Career History: You're in the 11 second zone!

We always look for the company name and positions on the **left** and the dates aligned on the **right** and in **bold** font. *Read that again - it's a really important point.*

Here's An Example:

ABC Company, Account Executive **January 2014 – Present**

Months should always be spelled out, to make your resume more complete. We look for consistency in dates as well. When one positions ends, the next one should start soon after. If there *are* gaps - then you need to fill in what you were doing at that point in time.

Following the company name, position title and dates will be a 1 – 3 sentence overview of your role. (More on the "how to" on this one a bit later in the chapter. Keep reading!)

Being able to describe your position in a **succinct manner** is probably the most **valuable exercise in writing a resume as it makes your interview shine!**

Most people stumble and ramble all over the place in trying to describe what they do. (Yes, we'll go through the "how to" on this one too!)

If you're an experienced professional, **career history must start on the first page**. If you're a recent college or university graduate, I recommend leading with education *before* career history.

2. Education: You're in the 11 Second Zone!

I've got fond memories of living on a student budget. Instant noodle soup, black coffee and cheap carbs...oh, and my dad's homemade wine were all staples that got me through post-secondary school.

Many positions have specific educational requirements. So, highlight your educational background clearly.

Start with post-secondary and work backward to high school. Again, reverse chronological order. Post-secondary out ranks high school, so it goes first.

Remember, if high school was more than 10 years ago, *leave off the year of graduation*. If you leave it, you're just sharing your age. *And, that needs to be kept your little secret.*

Indicate if your degree, diploma or certificate was awarded, otherwise we assume you didn't graduate. If you've got the paper be sure everyone knows it.

We also only need to know the graduation. We don't need the start and end dates.

Here's A Shiny Example:

EDUCATION:
University of Calgary, Bachelor of Arts, Degree Awarded, 2022
Red Deer College, Business Administration, Diploma Awarded, 2020
Harry Collinge High School, Diploma Awarded, 2019

If scholarships were awarded, do include them.

If there are a lot of awards, add a section called, AWARDS. If you received an off the charts GPA, note that detail as well!

If you've caught a hiring manager or recruiter's attention with your career history and your education, there's a good chance that the following section will get a SKIM.

5. Professional Development, Certifications, Associations:

You can use one or all of the above in this category.

Professional Development:

- Include specific courses
- Note specific professional certifications attained.

Professional Associations:

- Include memberships in Professional Associations

These last 4 sections will get SKIMMED if your resume is in the Top 20% pile.

6. Interests: Make Sure It's Interesting!

OK – now I'm going to say something that isn't meant to hurt your feelings.

I know you probably have many interests like gardening, cooking, reading, hiking, etc.

They are fun and interesting to YOU but not to an employer or recruiter. Why? It isn't all that interesting to us. We see the same few interests over and over – it doesn't stand out, so we just gloss over.

However, if you've completed five marathons, jumped out of an airplane, travelled to several countries, taken cooking classes around the world, self-taught a language, etc. *these are* interesting things to an employer or recruiter. Why? Because they stand out. They're unique and different vs. the same boring stuff that's typically listed.

A candidate I recently worked with shared she'd been the general contractor for a multi-year home renovation on her house. The hiring manager zoned in on that interest almost instantly. She knew how to use a tape measure, read blueprints and get dusty. All key requirements for the job she was applying for.

Don't shy away from the Interests section. It can be a game-changer for you!

Think about all of the *really cool stuff* you like to do in your leisure. Give your future employer a glimpse into what things you find fun. It shows your personality and character and THAT gives you an edge.

7. Volunteer Work: Show Us You Care

Volunteer work should always be included. It is a great strategy to showcase your philanthropic interests.

Be sure to indicate *how many hours per week* you volunteer, where you've volunteered, and specific achievements and accountabilities.

If you've volunteered 10 hours per week for the last 5 years that's a big commitment you'd want to highlight. *If you don't share, we could assume you volunteered for 1 hour over the past 5 years*. Yes, I just heard you gasp.

In Chapter 4, I'll explain the 2-step resume formula for your work history. Use the same formula to display your volunteer work.

8. Sports Achievements:

Athletic achievement *should always, always be included*. This is a significant area to have your resume stand out.

Why do we love seeing your sports achievements?

Athletics speak to many soft skills that employers are interested in such as: teamwork, competitiveness, leadership, desire to win, ability to lose graciously, ability to take on a rigorous training program, commitment and tenacity. These are all amazing skills to bring to a workplace!

9. Languages Spoken:

It may not be a requirement for the job, but it might be what tips the decision in your favour if two candidates are in a tie for the job.

10. Technical Skills:

If you're in a career where you have to be an expert in a specialized software or skill, you may want to include this section. It may not get read, but it will be key word searchable.

There you have it. We've *eased* **into the bones of your shiny resume.**

You know where the super shiny areas are and you've started to think about what makes those important parts stand out.

Get ready.

We're going to uncover your *Shiny Results.*

CHAPTER 4

Your Shiny Resume In 2 Quick Steps

Numbers, percentages and rankings make your resume a STAND OUT to employers and recruiters.

They get attention. And *you want attention.*

"There are two possible outcomes: The result confirms the hypothesis, then you've made a measurement.

If the result is contrary to the hypothesis, then you've made a discovery."

Enrico Fermi

Read that quote *twice*.

If you say you're GREAT at your job, your results will confirm that hypothesis. Easy.

But if the numbers don't prove you're GREAT at your job, you've just made a discovery on *what else should be measured in your resume.*

I've interviewed countless exceptionally talented candidates who have never considered outlining their shiny successes on their resumes.

I interviewed a stand out candidate this past summer. He was an articulate, professional sales candidate. I skimmed his resume and liked the type of companies he'd worked for, so we set up a time to meet.

At the end of our hour-long meeting, I discovered:

- He built a retail portfolio in excess of 4 million dollars annually through building a client base of over 1000 clients within 2 years.
- He sold uber high end electronics through cold calling up to 40 prospects per day, selling 100K+ systems.
- On a zero-entertainment budget, he secured ~900K in new business in less than 1 year.
- He was part of a team that sold fractional ownership of jets in excess of 26 million dollars. How cool is that?

And the list went on. **He was a star…CLEARLY!**

Once we uncovered these amazing results, I smiled and said,

"Hmmm, do you think I would know about these out-of-the-park results by reading your current resume?"

You guessed it.

Not ONE of the above results was on his first draft resume. We sure shone it up after that first meeting!

Let's dive into making *your resume* glisten with shiny numbers.

And we'll DITCH the bullets. I heard you GASP. Yes, it's time for you to release those suckers.

You're about to do the shiny 2-Step!

My SHINY 2-Step Resume Formula:

Here's the secret.

Once you nail this 2-STEP formula on your resume, interviews become EASY. In fact, you'll LOVE interviewing.

You'll clearly be able to describe what your roles are/were and you'll be armed with all sorts of sparkling details about your achievements.

The 2-step resume formula works if you're brand-new to your career or if you're a seasoned senior executive. It's all about results, no matter what your career or level.

A hiring manager seeks to understand only 2 things about each of your previous positions:

1. **Succinctly, *what was your role.***
2. **How *well* did you do in each role.**

A future company buys your previous results and successes.

If you've been successful in each of your past roles, odds are you plan to continue to be successful. **You're not going from a star to a dud now, are you?** Sounds silly, but it's true.

If you can show you've been an achiever in each of your past roles, well...*you become the candidate that's really easy to be hired.*

STEP 1: Create a SUMMARY of each role vs. a long list of bullets

It's time for you to get short, sweet and to the point. 1 – 3 sentences.

I'm going to show you exactly how to carefully craft a few sentences to make it clear what your role is/was.

All you have to do is answer 4 simple questions to create a succinct step 1 summary.

Your Step 1 Questions:

What level did you report to?

What is/was your job?

What was your scope?

How many other people did the same job?

When you answer these 4 questions, it becomes *crystal clear* what your role entailed.

You've hit the BIG SHINY MOMENT! Ahhhh.

Here's some examples of Step 1:

Reporting to the Canadian Vice President of Sales, I'm accountable for developing a net new book of business within an assigned territory in Calgary.

Reporting to the Division Director, I was the Administrative Assistant for the Director and her team of 5 Managers.

Reporting to the Warehouse Manager, I'm accountable for a team of 20-day shift Material Handlers. Responsible for scheduling, performance management, safety and production.

Reporting to the Accounts Receivable Manager, I'm part of a 5-person team, accountable for daily entry & coding of all Canadian and USA invoices into SAP.

Reporting to the Office Manager, I'm part of a 5-person team, accountable for all incoming calls, greeting & signing in visitors and receiving all couriers.

Reporting to the Director of Operations, my direct reports include 4 employment counsellors, overseeing 2 programs (ESL for Newcomers & Workplace Readiness) for 2000 job seekers annually, with an annual budget of 300K.

Reporting to the Inflight Manager, I'm part of a 6-person crew accountable for 275 guests, including safely and exceptional experience on 10+ international flights per month.

Reporting to the restaurant manager, I'm part of a 25-person server team, accountable for delivering an exceptional guest dining experience.

Do this test to see if you've nailed Step 1:

Read the sentences to Grandma, a 5-year-old or a good friend.

If they nod their head and say, *"I had no idea that's what your job was!"* – you've nailed it! Jackpot!

If their eyes glaze over with a look of confusion...*or boredom*, you haven't hit the sweet spot quite yet. Once you've passed the test, let's move on.

One to three sentences maximum. Keep it simple and powerful.

Let's get on to the good stuff.

STEP 2: Show your Shiny Results

This is what makes your phone ring.

What's shiny??

It's *all* about your amazing RESULTS and ACHIEVEMENTS.

It's *all* about the numbers.

The MAGIC lies in answering 3 BIG questions to create your SHINY results.

Your Step 2 Questions

To Uncover Your SHINY Results:

How big?

How much?

How many?

Before you delete all of the mind-numbing bullets on your current rusty resume, ask yourself:

What can I measure in these boring functional job responsibility bullets?

How big? How much? How many?

Chances are, you can turn those stinky bullets into something shiny.

Dig for numbers.

Step 2 is all about YOUR KEY SUCCESSES and KEY ACHIEVEMENTS!

Step 2 is what gives your resume *rocket-booster power*!

Before we dive in, here's a sneak peek on how a finished Step 2 will look.

The Step 2 on your resume will have **BULLETS**. *(Yes – **in this section** bullets are GOOD).*

SECRET: Bullets *do get read* if they're used under a heading that *screams:*

THERE'S SOMETHING IMPORTANT TO READ HERE.

Employers and recruiters will take note **there's important stuff to read** if you use one of these **magic headings**:

Key Successes

Key Achievements

You bullet each success or achievement.

Why does this work? Simple.

By bolding/underlining the beautiful words above, you tell the reader there's **shiny**, important, cool, validated stuff to read below the sub heading.

It catches their attention. Big time.

And, while we might still be in the initial SKIM phase of the 11 seconds, you've just put another few seconds into the ***SKIM bank account***.

As a recruiter– when I see this stuff I slow right down to take in the numbers and percentages you've outlined.

Outlining KEY SUCCESSES/ACHIEVEMENTS in each role tells me you've got a track record of being successful.

Hiring managers and recruiters *want to talk to candidates* who have a history of being successful.

As I've said earlier, a hiring manager buys your previous results.

If you've been successful in the past, odds are you'll find ways to stay successful. You become EASY to hire, because you've shown a strong track record of achievement.

Wait a second....

Is that your phone ringing?

13 Shiny Success Ideas To Get Your Wheels Turning:

Remember – numbers are *shiny!* Let's create some shiny bullets for you.

Get your pen out and start jotting down all of the areas you've excelled in.

Here are some ideas:

1. Attendance – did you have 100% attendance in the last year? Two years? Longer?

2. Accuracy in your work – do you have specific targets for quality? Did you achieve those targets? Or exceed them?

3. Have you been promoted? Was it in record time?

4. Have you been asked to take on additional responsibilities? If so, why?

5. Have you been asked to formally or informally train or mentor others?

6. How well did you do against any measurable targets? (HINT – look at your last performance review if you have one. There are loads of GEMS in those written reviews.)

7. Were you recognized by your peers or leadership with awards or accolades?

8. Did you bring forward any ideas that were implemented?

9. What were your rankings/grades on any professional development courses?

10. Were you selected for a special project? If so, out of how many people?

11. Where did your performance rank amongst others in the same role?

12. What can you validate with numbers or percentages?

13. What did you do that was above and beyond your basic role?

The ideas should be flowing!

Are you grinning ear to ear? You're probably realizing you have loads of great results to share. You just never thought of it this way before.

You're probably kicking yourself in the behind for missing these shiny details from your resume all of this time.

It's also probably become clear why your phone hasn't been ringing.

If you look up, likely there's a light bulb over your head. GRIN.

11 Shiny Success Ideas If You're New To Your Career:

I've presented what I lovingly call *"The Zippy Gig"* seminar to loads of new college and university graduates over the years.

When I talk about Step 2 of the resume process, I always see a *little panic* come over their faces. They worry that they don't have any shiny results because they're so new to the workforce.

You can feel the relief in the crowd when I share these SHINY SUCCESS IDEAS.

Let's get your creativity flowing:

1. 100% attendance in the last two years
2. Worked 20 hours per week while maintaining a full course load.
3. Volunteered 10 hours per week for the past year.
4. Secured the Coordinator role out of 200 applicants.
5. Nominated by peers for XX.
6. Achieved a 3.99 GPA.

7. Nominated for the Student of the Year.

8. Recognized with the XX Scholarship.

9. Received the highest grade in XX course out of XX classmates.

10. Consistently exceeded nightly beverage sales goals.

11. Ate 1460 cans of Campbell's soup while in school. Ha – just making sure you're paying attention!

Shiny Success Ideas For Sales Professionals:

If you're in sales and you don't have any numbers or percentages on your resume...

Burn it. Get out your BBQ lighter and set that resume on fire. Now.

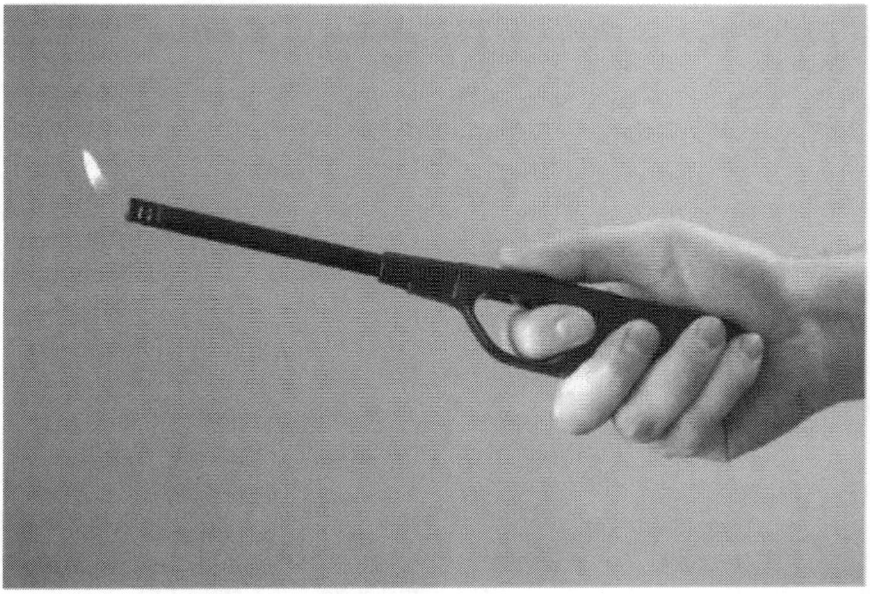

In sales *everything is measured*. If it's measured and it showcases what a star you are, include it.

Here are 8 ideas:

1. Built account base from zero to $XX.

2. Grew revenue in assigned accounts from $X to $Y.

3. Rankings within the sales team – ranked #1 out of 150 reps within 6 months.

4. Honoured with Presidents Club for exceeding annual plan by 250%.

5. Secured 15 new accounts in the first quarter of 20XX, exceeding my target by 50%.

6. Nominated by peers for the XX award!

7. Won a 2.5 Million RFP, representing the largest win in Canada in 20XX.

8. Promoted to Senior Account Executive within 6 months.

Shiny Success Ideas For 10 Distinct Careers:

I've had the pleasure of training a number of post-secondary school career services departments. One school in particular is a massive poly tech institution with a vast array of programs. I went through every program to show there's something to measure in every career discipline! Here's some ideas to get the wheels turning!

Administrative Assistant:

How many calls do you take per day? To how many memorized extensions?
How many proposals do you write? How many were successful? What was the dollar value? What was your accuracy rate?
How many board meetings do you organize per year? How many attendees? From how many cities?
How many people do you support? What are their titles?
How many visitors do you check in per day? How many couriers do you send or receive?
Have you been promoted? After what amount of time?

Human Resources:

How many people within the organization?
How many benefits claims, payroll or WCB matters do you handle?
How many performance reviews/performance improvement plans do you handle?
How many managers do you support?
How many hires do you make per month, quarter or year? What was the biggest recruit you've handled?
What's your department budget? Did you adhere to it?

Travel/Tourism:

How many clients do you work with per week?
How many trips do you book per day or week?
What was your most complex trip? How many flights/countries/duration?
Do you have $$ targets? If so, what was your actual $$ versus target?
Accuracy is key. (If I need a flight to Paris, France and I end up in Paris, Ontario, Canada...well, let's just say, I won't be happy!) What's your accuracy rating?

Customer Service: (Retail, hospitality, banking, etc.)

How many clients do you handle per day?
Targets versus actual on: customer service ratings, customers served per hour or sales $$ per day. Did you top the team on rankings? What was your best day?
Were you asked to train or mentor others? If so, how many? And, over what period of time?

Information Technology & Project Management:

How big was the project – dollar value, number of people on the project. Was it completed on time? On budget?
What was your most complex project? Time, dollars and result.
Most complex coding project? How many lines of code?
How many hours per week are you adding to your knowledge base to keep current?

Medical/Dental/EMT:

How many patients do you see per day?
How much time do you have to get a patient in/out? Are you hitting targets?
In a medical emergency, how many minutes do you have to assess the patient?

Finance:

How many transactions do you process daily, weekly? Against target or standard?
What's your accuracy rate (against target).
How many account codes do you have memorized? Accuracy rate?
How many collection calls do you make daily? What's your success rate?
Number of reports created – in what timeframe and accuracy?

Chef:

How many appetizers or meals do you produce each shift? Accuracy? Return rate?
What's the timeframe from order to delivery? Actual versus target?
Are you managing a budget? If so, were you on budget? Have you found cost-savings?

Trades

Safety track record – how long have you gone without a workplace incident?
What was the biggest project you worked on? Dollar value, # of people on your crew. How many floors or square feet? On time? On budget?
How quickly did you receive your tickets?

Appliance/Technical Repair

How many calls per day versus target?
How many types of appliances are you an expert at troubleshooting?
Customer Service ratings versus target?

The details count.

Here's What A SHINY Resume Looks Like!

When you put the 2-step formula together, the result is a crisp, clear shiny resume, glistening with your amazing results.

It is easy to read and understand.

I know immediately that you've been successful.

Here's a Shiny Resume Example:

ABC Company, Account Executive **January 2020 - Present**

Reporting to the Canadian Director of Sales, I was the sole representative for Calgary, responsible for developing new business through consistent cold calling efforts, networking and targeted creative marketing strategies.

Key Successes:

- Ranked in the top 10% in Canada out of 100 Reps.
- Delivered 150% over annual plan.
- Secured 52 new clients in 12 months.

WOW. WOW. WOW.

And, how powerful will your resume look once you add your key successes with #'s and %'s in each and every role?

Remember back to the rusty version of this resume? I had NO idea your amazing results were hidden in the rusty old thing.

I'd be tripping over myself to call you before another company scoops you up!

Remember. SHINY gets ATTENTION.

HEY!

Something cool just happened!

Do you know what it is?

You just made it through the tough part!

VOILA!!

You have a SHINY new resume that's *going to get results*.

And, this hard work will pay off BIG time, because you've now done most of the work needed to **nail the interview. (More on that coming up!)**

I'm so proud of you.

I may even have a tear in my eye.

CHAPTER 5
Lightning Round of Resume Tips

You've done all the hard work to make your resume shiny – congratulations!

Copyright © Sheila Musgrove

Now we'll add a few more sparkling ideas to take your resume right to the top 20% of resumes that get past the 11 second skim.

Hold on, grab your cup of java and read!

1. Don't Reveal The Private Stuff. EVER.
(Yes, we still see this everyday but we don't want to.)

- SIN number
- Marital status
- Date of birth

- Number of children/dependents
- Age. (Remember back to the recommendations on email addresses – don't use your birth year. You're just telling everyone how old you are. No one needs to know and they legally can't ask before you're hired.)
- Medical conditions

Confidential information such as your SIN, marital status, date of birth and number of dependents can only be asked for payroll and benefits administration, **once you've been hired**.

2. Ditch The Cover Letter. Yes, you read that right.

Cover letters rarely get read.

The only time I recommend writing one is *if it is specifically requested.* Otherwise **assume your cover letter won't be read**. In the rare instance you do need a cover letter, anything important in the letter such as results or your contact details, also needs to appear on your resume.

And, a little cover letter secret. When you upload your resume (and cover letter) to an ATS (applicant tracking system), remember - it's a pretty smart system. It distinguishes between your resume and cover letter and it tucks both documents into separate compartments. When a hiring manager is skimming through resumes, they ONLY go to the resume tab for the initial screen. They NEVER go to your cover letter... unless it's specifically been requested.

(Dash over to Chapter 6 on career pivots for a *sneaky secret on how to get your cover letter read.*)

3. Grammar Counts.

Spelling mistakes can be a **DEAL BREAKER** on a resume.

People cringe when I tell them this little fact.

Even *one typo* can have your resume sent straight to the recycle bin.

That goes for both the resume as well as an email message.

Take your time. Re-read before sending. Get someone to proof read it for you.

Why is it so important? It shows whether you pay attention to detail or not. It also gives a hiring manager a glimpse into your level of business communication. If you'll be communicating with clients or suppliers, typos and grammar are deal breakers.

4. Don't highlight any part of your resume with a black background. I'll curse if I've accidentally printed your resume and half of my ink cartridge gets drained.

5. Don't talk about yourself in the third person. <u>That's just WEIRD.</u>

6. Think Key-Word Searchable:

Many companies and recruitment firms use their ATS system to rank candidates based on the specific key words for the role.

You want to ensure their key words appear in your resume, so you rank higher and get a chance at the first 11 second SKIM.

The key words are in the job posting. Scan the posting for the "must have" requirements and ensure those words are in your resume.

If you look carefully at job postings, you'll often see at the very bottom a note that reads, "Key Words". As much as you're trying to be noticed by employers, they also want *you to find them and their job postings.*

Often employers dissect the role and use multiple words or phrases that don't appear in the posting as they could be words/phrases you're using in your resume.

There are multiple titles that can be used, so if we're looking for an Account Manager, we might also add key words such as: Account Rep, Account Exec, Account Executive, Sales Rep, Territory Rep, Business Development Rep, Business Development Manager, Sales Representative.

It's just another way to ensure that we find each other!

I know. That was a *really* good tip!!

Applying via Email: Don't Make These Critical Mistakes

You've got your shiny new resume in hand and you're **ready to start applying for *ZIPPY GIGS***.

Imagine all of the work you've done to change your resume from rusty to shiny and then...you do an epic fail?

The EPIC FAIL:

Sending your resume WITHOUT TYPING ONE SINGLE word in the email.

Seriously?

That's like phoning someone, having your name and number displayed, but not saying a word when the person answers. Just lots of heavy breathing.

You'd never do it. It would be silly. And rude. And weird.

As the person receiving the call, I know it's you phoning, but I have no idea if you're in trouble, want to invite me for wine or you're just calling to say hello.

So, why would you send a blank email with your beautiful shiny resume without at least saying hello?

An email is a PROFESSIONAL piece of communication that's vital when applying for a job.

This is yet another way to stand out and make an impression. Positively or negatively.

A positive impression is made when you show you can construct a proper email, including words! GRIN.

Subject Line: Job Title or Job Number...or both

Email Body: Greeting, message and close

Here's a Shiny Example:

> Hello Sheila,
>
> Enclosed please find my resume for your consideration for the Account Executive role.
>
> I am an experienced business development representative with 5 years of exceptional results along with a degree in Commerce from the University of Calgary. I was excited to read your posting and feel that I would be a great fit with TAG Recruitment.
>
> I would welcome the opportunity to meet for an interview. I can be reached at: 403-237-5656.
>
> Very best,
>
> Amber Wilson

Don't fret about the greeting and closing options. Keep it simple.

Greeting Options:

Dear Sheila
Hello Sheila
Hi Sheila
Sheila,

Closing Options:

Thank you,
Very best,
Best,
Sincerely,
Best regards,
Yours truly,

The greeting and closing in an email can be a little less formal than what's expected in a formal business letter.

The only closing I'm not fond of is **"Cheers".**

You're applying for a job, not making a toast over a cocktail.

That's for later...when you get your shiny new *zippy gig*!

What Should You Put In The Subject Line Area?

When applying via email, also note the WORST subject line is "Resume". GRIN. Candidates always laugh when I point out I'm a recruiter. How many emails with the subject line "Resume" do you think I get each day?

The subject line should note the position title and/or competition number. If you were referred by someone, consider "Referred by Jane Smith".

When you attach your resume, ensure you've looked carefully at your file name.

HarrySmithVersion43 isn't a great name. GRIN.

It should simply be your name and perhaps a month. That's it.

P.S. And always double check to ensure you've attached the correct document.

And, the last word on email. **Use your own email. Yes, <u>yours.</u>**

It's just ***silly*** to open an email from Kate Smith only to see a note and resume from Eddy Whyte.

Eddy, my friend, get *your own* email address.

OK, you're probably right. ***That was sassy***. Here it is:

CHAPTER 6

How To Do A Career Pivot...Without Getting Dizzy.

Yes...you can change careers. At any stage of your life.

There are many reasons why you might be considering a pivot to a new career. And they are all worthy!

Perhaps...

- there's a change in the economy and your former career is no longer in demand.
- you may be bored to tears with your job and need a BIG change.
- you want to contribute to society in a more meaningful way
- you've decided now is the time to earn a better income.
- you went to school for a specific career, but now realize it just isn't for you.

I get it. I've been there! My educational path is a bit of a zig zag. Clerk typist (yes, that was the actual title of the program), Legal Assistant and the topper...my degree is Law in the Liberal Arts, with a minor in Soviet East European Studies. Not quite the educational path for a business owner, recruiter, author & speaker.

No matter what your educational background is, you're not locked into a set career. Your education is just a springboard to launch your career in whatever direction you'd like. At any stage you'd like.

Whatever the reason, I've got a few steps to make your transition EASY.

"I wasn't destined to be an astronaut. I had to turn myself into one."

Chris Hadfield

First, you need to put some work into the change you seek. In a CTV interview a few years ago, I spoke with the anchor about career pivots. I made him chuckle when I said, *"I might love wine and a good party, but that doesn't give me the skill to be a stellar event planner."* GRIN.

You need more than a *burning desire* to leave your job and start something new. It takes some work to make a pivot successful.

But it is work absolutely worth doing.

You'll likely need to invest in education to gain new skills.

Look to volunteer opportunities to gain practical experience. Often overlooked are temporary or contract gigs.

"46% (of the global workforce) is planning to make a major career pivot or career transition."

Microsoft 2021 Work Trend Index

4 Pivot Tips & A Sneaky Secret:

1. **Education:** In most cases, you'll probably need to invest in a course or certification to make the switch to a new career. When you invest in education to bridge the pivot, your education needs to move to the top of your resume. It helps an employer make sense of your new career direction.

2. **Volunteer work:** Volunteering is a great strategy to help gain experience in your newly chosen field of work. Follow the same 2-step resume formula as described in chapter 4 to showcase your experience, again with emphasis on successes and achievements. If you're not working, add your volunteer work in with your work history. This helps show you're firmly committed to a new career direction.

3. **Target position:** This is an absolute must-have when you pivot. Back in Chapter 1, I shared how resumes are read in those first critical 11 seconds. We skim. Company name & title, education, where are you located and #s and %'s. That's it. You've got one shot.

If you're a geologist and you've applied for an event coordinator role, I'll think you've goofed up and applied for the wrong role. So, I'll glance the top of your resume to see your "target position". If you have the exact title of the role you're applying on, then I know it's not a mistake. I then glance at the next section on your resume, EDUCATION and I'll see you've taken courses to segue to your new career. Without a target position (or education) at the top of your resume, the odds are high I'll just move on.

4. **Yes, your previous background still matters**. I still want to see your successes from your previous career. If you were successful in your previous work, of course you're going to continue to try to excel in your new career. You'll take all sorts of transferrable skills from your old career to your new one.

No matter what your previous career was, if you were successful in the past, you'll pour that same work ethic and desire to do a great job into your new career.

"Find something you're passionate about and keep tremendously interested in it."

Julia Child

<u>Lastly, here's that sneaky tip.</u>

As you read earlier, I'm not a fan of cover letters because they all read the same and don't tell me anything juicy about your background.

And, when you upload to an ATS system, it's smart enough to know which document is your resume and which is the cover letter. It tucks those two documents in *completely different sections*, so the hiring manager doesn't have to sift through documents they're not interested in reading. (We all hate the cover letter.)

BUT, in a big career pivot you should explain the "why". Why are you making a career pivot and why did you choose this new career path? The cover letter is where you'd explain those details.

Here's how to get your cover letter read...or at least glanced at!

Rather than saving your cover letter as a separate document, *save it as the first page of your resume*. Of course, the hiring manager will open your resume document, and voila, it's going to get a quick glance.

Now, I may be a bit annoyed that you've tricked me into reading your cover letter, so keep it brief and to the point. You need to be a bit punchy with your subject line, but not too outrageous.

Here's some examples:

RE: Geologist Turned Event Planner

RE: Accountant Transforms Into Executive Assistant

RE: Career Pivot: Sales Manager to Executive Director

Keep the letter brief and to the point. *The goal is to quickly answer the "why".* Why are you changing careers? And, what have you done to make a smooth transition to your new career? Focus on education and volunteer work.

In the initial phone screen, the top question will be, "Why are you choosing this new career path?" Plan what you'll say and rehearse it out loud. If you skimmed over the interviewing chapter (chapter 9), dash back and read why it's sooooooo important to rehearse out loud.

You'll thank me for it.

Here's some high-profile career pivoters to give some inspiration:

1. Vera Wang was a figure skater and journalist before becoming a gown designer.

2. Julia Child was in advertising before writing her first cookbook.

3. Brad Pitt was a limo driver and mascot before launching into acting.

If Brad Pitt can drive a limo and wear a chicken costume...

I'm pretty sure you've got an excellent chance of changing your career too. GRIN.

CHAPTER 7
The Big T – Terminations & Other Tough Conversations

Have You Been Canned Like My Mom's Beets?

My mom, Betty, makes the most AMAZING canned pickled beets each fall.

It looks positively dangerous to me with the big canner on the stove filled with boiling water. The result is so worth it. My mom has purple hands, purple tea towels, purple countertops and there's a big reason why.

Canned beets are delectable little morsels. And, Betty loves to make them.

But there's also a canning that isn't so delectable.

Did your stomach just go into a little knot? I'm just going to say it.

You were canned. Terminated. Turfed. Ousted. Fired. #ohshit

The BIG T.

Hey. It happens. For lots of reasons.

I know you feel like crap about it and would love to stuff it under the rug of your resume.

Don't do that.

Why?

Because you *will* be asked about it.

Don't worry. I break it down step-by-step how to talk about this in an interview.

The Big T – 4 Steps To Face the "Were You Fired?" Question

1. **Own it.** Step right into it. What really happened? Before you even think about going to an interview, take some time to work through the Big T.

   Could you have done anything to change the outcome? If so, own that answer. Be accountable.

   After interviewing loads of candidates who have been faced with a Big T – there are ones that simply can't be explained.

Some examples are:

A new manager came in and cleaned house...leaving you without a job for no real reason.

The company was bought/sold and the team was shuffled.

The role changed and your skills were no longer aligning.

I've got some ideas for you in the next section as well, so don't fret.

2. **Write your answer to the inevitable question** – *Why did you leave XX company??* You want to avoid blaming the company and simply explain the scenario objectively.

3. **Rehearse the answer out loud.** Do you sound positive? Are you explaining the reason rationally? Is it believable? Does your voice have any trace of bitterness?

4. **You're ready for interviewing when you don't dread answering the Big T question**. You've released the fear.

"Cows run away from the storm, while the buffalo charges toward it – to get through it quicker. Whenever I'm confronted with a tough challenge, I do not prolong the torment, I become the buffalo."

Wilma Mankiller, Principal Chief of the Cherokee Nation

Yup, it's a crappy spot to be in. Own it.
And be ready to talk about it in your next interview.

There are Really Only 6 Broad Reasons for The Big T:

1. **Performance.** This one is simple. You were hired to deliver specific results and you didn't. Own it. Know why.

Was there something going on in your personal life that took away attention from work?

Did the role change and you were no longer a fit?

Was there something in the economy that prevented you from delivering?

Was there a political power play going on in the organization?

Was it a technical issue? New software, tools, or technology that you couldn't/didn't learn?

Did you over inflate your skills in the interview? And, then, #ohshit you weren't able to do the job?

2. **Personality.** Perhaps you didn't mesh with your colleagues, management or your clients.

This one happens often. I met a talented fellow who had grown into a VP role over several years. A new CEO came in and she simply didn't like him. Over the course of several months, she just made his life difficult and then eventually decided to terminate his employment. It's unfortunate. But it happens. Sure, he was deflated when he came to see me. We fixed that in a hurry. We applied the 2-step resume formula to his resume. It was bursting with amazing results. He left my office with a spring in his step. Any hiring manager who read his resume could clearly see he was a star. And, the termination became a moot-point (and it was clear that it was just a personality misalignment. *Her loss, this guy was golden*!)

3. **Values misalignment.** I interviewed a designated accountant who was asked by the owners of the company to "fix" the books. He of course flat -out refused as he wasn't going to put his professional reputation or designation on the line. He was asked to leave that day.

Plain and simple. You were asked to do something that sent your moral compass spinning.

4. **Culture misalignment.** You just didn't fit.

A candidate I worked with shared a fun story. She worked as a weight loss consultant. She was also human and every now and then she craved a fast-food burger, which of course was a big no-no for the lunch room at her place of work. She disguised herself with big sunglasses, zipped through the drive through and then parked blocks away with her seat fully reclined so she wouldn't be spotted as she wolfed down her greasy fries and cheeseburger! Had that taken place daily, likely there would've been a culture misalignment.

5. **Something illegal or unethical happened.** We won't go into detail on this one. We should all have a good pulse on what is right and wrong.

6. **Showing up**. Perhaps you just forgot to keep going to work?

True story. It will give you a laugh!

I called a fellow who failed to show up for training in his first week on the job. The conversation went something like this:

Sheila: David, I just heard from Mary in HR, she said you haven't yet arrived for training this morning. Are you ok?

David: Yeah, my car broke down on the way. I'm just in a cab now.

Sheila: Oh, good, so you'll be at the office in 15 minutes?

David: Ummm, no. I'm going home.

Sheila: You had two options. Going home or going to work. Unfortunately, you picked the wrong one.

Sheila: David, the very best thing you can do when you get a job, is to go.

This is one of our TAG team's "go to phrases". And yes, that was David's last day of work.

"Storms make trees take deeper roots."

Dolly Parton

BIG T terminations happen.

Dust yourself off.

You CAN be a rock star in your next role.

You Were Laid Off? Breathe.

Let's clarify something in case you're feeling bad about something you shouldn't be.

Being laid off or going through a down size is a LAY OFF. *It's not a termination.*

Never refer to a lay off or downsize as a *termination* or *let go.*

Alarm bells go off in my head when I hear the words:

Let-go, Fired or Terminated

Only use these words *if they are true*. And if so, go back to the last section about The Big T and own your answer as to WHY it happened.

If you were laid off, that's different. It happens. Still shitty, but a different set of circumstances that only requires a brief explanation.

You just need to explain **what happened in the *organization***. Don't assume the hiring manager knows why the lay-offs took place. Tell the story.

Example:

The province was in a recession and the company's volumes decreased by 500% in the last quarter.

Give the larger picture.

How many people were laid off? Where you in the first, second or third round of layoffs? *(Keep in mind: How Big, How Many, How Much?)*

The scope gives me an idea of magnitude. If you were the only person in the entire company of 400 people that was laid off, I'll dig deeper.

If you were in the last round of lay-offs, helping to close down the company with the president, I'd think you were a keeper. They really didn't want to let you go.

Tell me the story.

Big T terminations are really crappy career moments. No sugar coating this one.

They also happen to talented, hard-working, good people. I've interviewed LOADS of them.

A termination isn't going to define the rest of your career. *Read that sentence again.* It's not going to define your career. You WILL get past this *not-so-great* career moment.

Own it. Be prepared to talk about it objectively in an interview. Lay-offs are also crappy moments. They happen. Tell the story of what happened in the company. You'll get past these career bumps, too.

Please know another company will find your skills and background to be a perfect fit.

"Careers are a jungle gym, not a ladder."

Sheryl Sandberg

CHAPTER 8

Clever Ways To Cover Gaps In Your Resume

I'll be blunt.

Hiring managers and recruiters don't like gaps on your resume.

Our ideal?

When one position stops another should *immediately* start again. Your resume only shows month and year, so if you took a week or two before starting your next role, that's still considered immediate. Even if you had a month off before starting a new role, you'll still be fine. A gap is anything beyond a couple of months.

But, let's get real.

Life happens.

Stuff happens.

And, back-to-back positions aren't always possible.

Here's a secret to overcome your resume gaps.

Use a placeholder with start and end dates (or to present), just like a regular job. Yes – you're stepping right into the GAP and giving it a name!

Whatever has taken you away from your career, you're not sitting back binge-watching Netflix. You're doing stuff.

7 Placeholder Ideas For Gaps:

1. Sabbatical. Yes, it's normally used in academia as a term to say you're off doing research. It's really a career pause. Sure, you'll have to explain what the heck you mean by a "sabbatical" during the phone screen, but it will get you one step closer to a conversation.

It can cover many things. Maybe you were moving to a new province or country and decided to blend in some travelling. Maybe it was a full-on travel sabbatical with a bit of work tossed in. **The point is, you were off doing something**. *(You haven't been binge-watching Netflix the entire time.)* That "something" probably gave you some incredible new skills a future employer may find fascinating.

2. Caregiver Responsibilities. Did you care for children, a spouse, parent or other loved one? It's a full-time job. Good for you for being there. You had schedules and appointments to keep. Medications to keep track of. No apology needed. This is a tough job and says much about your character.

3. Out of Country Responsibilities. Maybe you had to return to your home country for family or business. That's ok too.

4. Career Pivot: Dash over to Chapter 6 for all the juicy details on how to do a successful career pivot. You can refer to the education or training you've taken to pivot to your new career and/or the volunteer work you've done to gain experience.

5. Covid Lay Off. Some of my coaching clients have had a lot of fun with this section on their resume. They've listed all sorts of amazing successes/achievements such as:

Started a fitness routine - lost 40 pounds.

Self-taught via You Tube how to install hardwood flooring in their home.

Took 20 on-line courses.

6. Entrepreneurial Pursuits. I get it. You had a burning passion to be in business for yourself. You needed to give it a try! You took a different direction in your career. It's absolutely OK to list on your resume as it shows initiative.

7. Gap Year. Rather than dashing straight from high school to college or university, you chose to take a gap year to travel. You'll have loads of great experiences to share on your resume and in job interviews. Chances are you did various work-abroad positions to round out your experience.

One of my best hires at TAG was a world-traveler. He'd lived in multiple countries and gained tremendous work experience (mostly all outside of recruitment). He was an easy hire as he demonstrated he was resilient, adaptable to changing situations and at ease with the unknown.

"88% of gap year graduates reported that their Gap Year improved their employability. 60% reported that it helped them define their career path."

American Gap Year Association Survey

Here's Some Examples:

Travel & Working Abroad	**September 2019 – February 2022**
Upon securing my work visa, I moved to New Zealand, where I took the first three months to explore the country and culture, before securing two, long-term contracts in the financial services sector.	

Covid Lay Off **June 2020 to March 2021**

Due to the pandemic mandatory restaurant closures, my former employer shut down all 5 Alberta locations.

Key Successes:

- Started a fitness program and lost 20 pounds.
- Via You Tube, I self-taught how to lay 1000 square feet of hardwood in my home.
- Took 15 on-line general-interest courses.

Whenever I deliver my *Zippy Gig Seminar*, I'm always asked about unusual gaps.

One woman told me she had a 3-year gap on her resume due to a critical illness. Bless her heart – she wasn't taking it sitting down.

While going through treatment, she enrolled in college to take a program in social work. She wanted to be able to counsel others who were undergoing treatment and use both her newfound professional experience with her personal journey.

Let's read that again – ***while going through extensive treatment,*** she enrolled in school.

Wow. I shared with her what she just told me about herself.

With that comment she told me *she's resilient.* I needed a tissue. We both had tears in our eyes. I hugged her and said she had *nothing to worry about.*

A future employer would be LUCKY to have her strength.

Life happens. Curveballs happen to all of us.

And like the incredibly resilient woman, **think about all of the amazing things your resume tells me about how you've handled the curveball.**

Own it all. It will feel good.

"The only thing that ever sat its way to success was a hen."

Sarah Brown

CHAPTER 9

Rock Your Interview

I started running a few years ago when I moved into the city.

A beautiful park is close by and the running paths along the Bow River are just a few kilometres away. When I started running, it was just purely for cardio and general exercise.

I had no intentions of running in an actual race....

...until a very cute guy was involved.

He texted on a Friday night to casually say,

"Hey, let's run a 10K race on Sunday morning."

OMG – I panicked.

I ran regularly, but seriously 10K? I'd never run 10K before.

And, I only had a day and a half to get ready to run. Well, I thought, why the heck not?

I was nervous as hell. The race went just fine. Even though I ran off course – not once, but twice. And, I'd also convinced other people to come with me. Yes, I sure did.

I finished the race in one piece, with a fairly respectable time considering my silly detours.

And, the best part was the handsome man jumping up and down to hug me at the finish line. GRIN.

I did another 10K a few months later, and I started to dabble thoughts about running a half marathon.

After dinner one January night, my pal Cyndi gave me her training schedule for an April race. I taped it to the inside of my pantry and then just started to train. I ended up injured right before that race, which happens when you're a 40 something training for your first half marathon.

So, I chose a new goal. The Calgary Half Marathon.

Training to run 21.1K takes time and commitment.

It's like creating a shiny resume and preparing for an interview.

The thought of running straight for a couple of hours seemed insane. But I did it...with lots of effort.

I'd dial in a great play list with some get-your-ass-in-gear music and I'd say to myself,

'Just get started – put one foot in front of the other and just get going.'

My legs and lungs were fine for a 2.5-hour training run.

But my HEAD was the problem.

#selfie

I had silly and random thoughts.

You know the little-bit-of-doubt that creeps in when you do something for the first time?

I can't possibly run 21.1K.
Why do I need to do this?
My legs will give out.
Goodness sakes, I could have a heart attack.
I can't feel my heart beating.
Why am I wearing an orange tank top and a purple jacket?
My toes are numb.
I think I'm going to run out of water.
Why did I drink so much water?
I have to pee and I have 5K left.
I think my hamstrings are seizing.
OMG my ass is seizing.
Am I passing out?
Those geese look mean.
That goose could take me down.
OMG the goose is chasing me.
I'm almost done.
I should run a full marathon.
I run like the wind.
Yay, I'm done!
I feel GREAT. OK, my feet hurt. And my legs. And hips.
But this was sooooo worth it.

What DOUBTS are in your head about Interviewing?

You probably have many of the same thoughts I had about running.

The list looks surprisingly similar...ok, except the part about the geese.

I can't possibly get that job.
Why do I need a new job?
I don't have the skills for that job.
Interviewing is painful.
I could have a heart attack. *(I'm sure this has never happened in an interview)*
Why did I wear this suit? I should have worn the black suit.
My hands are sweating.
My mouth is dry.
I have to pee.
My legs could give out.
I could pass out.
The hiring manager looks mean.
She's going to ask tough questions.
This is uncomfortable.
Oh gawd, we're starting.
OK, this isn't so bad.
Yay, I aced the interview!
I'm sooooo getting an offer.
I love interviewing. I'm a star!

Isn't it strange how we have these crazy random thoughts?

Sassy Sheila Advice: Get your head into a different space.

99% of the hiring managers you meet – WANT to find every reason to HIRE you. *You just have to help them to be right.*

Read it again. Doesn't that feel like a much nicer mental space to walk into an interview with?

It's true. I love sharing this in my keynotes. I can see the weight lifting off the shoulders of the attendees. Most hiring managers want to get back to their regular work and stop interviewing. Most aren't interested in interviewing for sport. They need to fill the position, get you started and trained so they can continue reaching their goals.

One quick point before we dive into the interview process – let's talk about the casual phone chat.

Here's the truth – it's not a casual phone chat.

It's a mini-interview.

Before we invest an hour of our time for a formal interview, we want to ensure the role in question could be a good fit. So, we book a 5-minute phone appointment with you first.

In our 5-minute conversation I'm assessing:

Your phone manner – energy, enthusiasm, interest level, tone, grammar, vocabulary and overall communication skills.

If your phone rings when you're in a noisy restaurant or while you're driving down the highway or.... the call woke you up from a nap...**DON'T take the call**. If you can't be at your razor-sharp best, let the call go to voicemail. Call back when you're in a quiet space and you can give the phone interview your absolute best.

Your interest and alignment to the role. I've liked what I've read on your resume. I'm listening to hear if what you're saying aligns to your resume.

I will be bold and also ask you your **current and future target income.** Yes, that might seem direct, but I want to ensure we're in the same range. It wouldn't be fair to ask you to spend an hour in an interview with me if the salary wasn't even close to what you hoped for.

I'll certainly tell you a bit more about the role and who the role is with (if working with an agency recruiter – we want to ensure you haven't applied for the role already). I'm gauging if this really is the type of role that gets you hopping out of the bed in the morning.

Do you have the **skills and background** (at a high level) to be a solid candidate for the role?

If I have a deadline for the role, **does our timing work**?

If you are a "yes" to the above, chances are you'll be invited for an interview.

Sidebar funny story: After doing a routine pre-screen interview with a candidate, I invited him for an interview and confirmed the necessary details on when and where. He was booked. He passed the mini- interview. Thennnnnn, he kept talking. He said, *"Wow, I'm so surprised you asked me for an interview!! I thought I totally screwed up that earlier question."* Once you're invited for the interview, ensure you don't talk yourself out of the invitation.

You've got every chance to rock the interview and get the Zippy Gig. But you have to prepare.

2 BIG "Must-do's" To Prepare For Your Interview:

The worst thing you can do is walk into an interview and just "wing it". *Never do that.*

Yes, you're going to prepare.

An interview really is a sales presentation on YOU.

Think back to those dreaded public speaking moments in high school. If you're like me, I was terrified.

Chances are you stood nervously gripping cue cards and rehearsed your speech out loud. Of course, you did.

Think of your interview as an on-stage performance. You need to rehearse what you're going to say.

Copyright © Sheila Musgrove

1. Rehearse out loud. ***Why?***

It's a cool brain thing.

When you rehearse out loud – what you're saying is committed to short term memory. If a case of the nerves hit, your short-term memory kicks in and you can recall what you've rehearsed.

Here's the not-so-cool-thing.

If you haven't rehearsed out loud, everything on your resume is resting in your long-term memory.

And, if those nerves hit (let's say you expected one person in the interview and you walk into a panel of five people) your long- term memory is shot.

You get flustered. All of a sudden you can't remember what role you were in 5 years ago. Hell – you can't even remember your name. And, the interview is blown.

If you say,

"*Can I see my resume, so I can remember*?".

Your interview is now done. Cooked. Oh-so-over.

You've just told me that you don't have a memory.

You can't even remember your background?

That's not a good thing.

Rehearse walking through your resume several times. Once doesn't cut it.

2. Know your career history off the top of your head.

I've said to many a nervous candidate,

"You're not convincing me that you even know your own background."

Why? They fumble around, get mixed up – it's like they're trying to convince me they are someone else (and doing a very bad job I might add).

Here's an easy rule. Plan what you'll say *in advance*.

You might think, '*Yeah, that's great, but I still have no idea what to say!*'

Not to worry, those answers are coming up.

4 Ways Your Most Critical Interview Question Will Be Asked:

Most candidates would rather go to the dentist for a root canal than go to an interview.

I'm going to change your mind on this one, sunshine.

You'll love interviewing once you know what to expect.

So Where Does Interview Anxiety Come From?

The anxiety for most candidates comes when they realize they have to highlight virtually everything on their resume.

And, if you didn't create a shiny resume, it's terrifying to think about how the heck you can talk about the bullets.

But, you're super smart. And, you've created a SHINY resume. So, this part is going to be EASY for you.

Pssst. Want to know a secret?

There's one question you'll be asked in EVERY interview.

It can be asked a few different ways, *but it's the exact same question.*

4 Variations of THE question that is ALWAYS asked:

1. Bring your resume to life for me.

2. Tell me about your current position.

3. Tell me about your previous position.

4. Walk me through your background.

This is where the *out-of-body experience* starts for most people.

Sheer fear of what the heck to talk about.

So, it starts.

The meandering ramble.

You feel your mouth moving but your brain sure isn't firing.

It's as painful for the interviewer to listen to as it is for you to deliver.

But it doesn't have to be like this.

GUESS WHAT?

If you've done a SHINY resume, you've already got a gold star because you can answer this MASTER question with ease.
You already have a few concise sentences from the STEP 1 preparation of your resume, so bringing your resume to life in the interview will be EASY!
Time yourself.

If you rattle through your resume in less than 5 minutes, that's waaaay too short. And, you're missing the important stuff.

If you're still spewing out words at the 45-minute mark, the interviewer deserves a gold medal for not throwing their pen at you. Kidding.

Stay Out Of The Weeds.

The BIG mistake most experienced candidates make in interviews is going into granular detail about your job.

The magic amount of time is 10 - 15 minutes. OK, maybe less than 10 minutes if you're new to your career.

10 – 15 minutes is ample time to SUCCINCTLY walk through your career history. The goal is for the hiring manager to understand (with ease) what your roles have been and where you've been successful.

Just like your resume needs white space, so does the interview. By white space, I mean explaining your career background clearly. If you go into the weeds, we're both going to be covered in mud by the end of the interview. HA. And, you don't want that.

You need to rehearse the sentences out loud and then you'll nail the BIG interview question – no matter how they throw it at you.

6 Things An Interviewer Wants To Learn About Each Role:

Most candidates I work with tell me they have absolutely no idea what to say in an interview. And, they're right. They don't.

Once I start the interview, yup, the **deer-in-the-headlights** look appears on their face. You try to share a story about your background based on the 2 – 3 pages of bullets in your rusty resume. Words are coming out, but it sounds like a ***meandering-out-of-body experience***. GRIN.

I guarantee that'll NEVER happen to you again!

Let me unravel the mystery.

6 things we're looking to learn from you:

1. Succinctly, what was the role & what were you accountable for?
2. What level did you report to?
3. How many people did the same role?
4. What's your scope?

5. How successful were you – yes, the *shiny numbers*.
6. Why did you leave or why are you looking to leave?

Look familiar? Of course, it does. GRIN.

It's the 2-step SHINY resume formula.

You've got all of the "answers" to the interview *test* on your resume.

All you have to do is rehearse out loud and you'll be a ROCKSTAR in your interview.

Those Dreaded "*Tell Me About A Time*" Questions:

These questions are dreaded by every candidate I've met.

The "tell me about a time" questions are called behavioural based questions.

The reason they're asked is simple.

Past performance and behaviours are the best indicators of your future performance.

I'll be honest. I'm not a fan of behavioural based questions. They tend to focus more on the negative than the positive. They're still used, so prepare for them.

You have loads of examples of achievements that can easily be woven into the answer to multiple behavioural based questions.
When creating Step 2 – the shiny results on your resume, I shared that a hiring manager is hiring your previous results.

Because if you've been successful in each of your last positions, chances are you'll continue to be successful.

With 2 or 3 pages of successes clearly noted on your resume, you're showing a hiring manager that you're a rockstar. I'll say it again – **you become REALLY easy to be the candidate who is hired because you've shown your past performance.**

"Sometimes the questions are complicated and the answers are simple."

Dr. Seuss

6 Behavioural-based Questions To Prepare For:

Tell me about a time...

1. When you went above and beyond? What was the result?

2. You had a conflict with a co-worker. What happened and how was it resolved?

3. When you brought a new idea to your manager. Was it implemented? Why or why not?

4. When you disagreed with a decision made by your manager?

5. You were recognized for outstanding work?

6. When you missed your performance targets. How did you get back on track?

The key to getting through these questions is to PREPARE. Take some time to think about examples to each of the questions above.

We want to hear the specific scenario and how you handled it.

It shows us more of who you are, your personality, how you handle difficult situations as well as how you create success.

Feeling the pressure? You won't if you take the time to prepare.

10 Additional Questions to Prepare For:

Sassy Sheila speaking here... *I think the dumbest question still asked is:*

1. Tell me about your strengths and weaknesses.

The answers are always the same, which is why I don't ask the question. But, lots of people still ask this silly question, so prepare for it.

Be a stand out with clever responses.

And I do mean *clever*.

Don't use worn-out RUSTY responses we've all heard.

My Strengths: I'm a team player. I love what I do. I'm really good at my job.

My Weaknesses: I take on too much. I care too much. I'm a perfectionist. I work too much.

BORING. OVER-USED. DULL. YAWNNNNN

You must bring your clever and shiny self!

My Strengths – simply tie to your shiny results and how you've been able to achieve them.

My Weaknesses – think about where you're stretching your performance to get to the next level in your career.

2. Where do you want to be professionally in the next 3 – 5 years?

If you've created a shiny resume, your target position is clear. Think about where you'd like to be in the position after this next one.

3. Tell me what you know about our company.

Research the company. You should know what the company does, a bit of history (when it was started), geographical locations, awards and perhaps who the executive team are, and what the company does of course.

4. What's your ideal job?

A job interview isn't the time to be wishy- washy. Give some thought to what your ideal job is. HINT – ***ideally, it's the one you're interviewing for***.

5. Tell me something about your background that I wouldn't know by reading your resume. (This is an opportunity to highlight a cool "interest").

I LOVE this question. If you've unearthed something really interesting for your "interests" section, this is the place to spotlight it.

6. What do you really like about your present job?

What's the juiciest part of your current gig? If you could amplify the great parts of your role, what are they?

7. What would you change about your present job?

We all have parts of our job that aren't our favourite. What are they for you? Keep it positive though.

8. Tell me about your biggest success or career milestone.

Pull one of your Step 2 Key Successes from your resume. (See, all of that work on creating a shiny resume is paying off BIG time.)

9. What was your biggest achievement in your last role?

GRIN. Yes, it's all on your SHINY resume.

10. Is there anything else you were hoping to cover?

I always end with this question – I want to ensure I haven't missed anything.

Write out your answers to these questions. Rehearse out loud. Own the answers. You're well on your way to ACING the interview.

But, wait! There's more. I've asked some top Canadian executives for their insight on favourite interview questions and what makes a candidate a stand-out.

9 Smart End of Interview Questions to Ask

You've made it through the interview. It went really well. Yay!!

Then a last question comes where the tables turn. The interviewer smiles, and asks...

What questions can I answer for you?

POOF!! *The Deer In Headlights Is Back!*

You MUST have a question or two ready.

And don't ask silly questions about salary. (More on that in a second!)

If you don't ask ANY questions, you look terrified and ill-prepared.

Not the best look for you nor does it leave a lasting impression.

NEVER Ask These Silly Questions:

1. What's the salary?
2. What are the benefits?
3. How many weeks of vacation?
4. When can I take my first vacation days?
5. Are sick days covered?
6. Do you close during the holiday season?
7. Is there a bonus?
8. Are salary increases given each year?

You get the point.

These are all about YOU. And, if you're more concerned about how much time you get to spend away from your job, I will likely de-select you as fast as you've uttered these questions.
Don't fret, all of these questions get answered at a later date, so don't ask them now.

I want you to up your game.

Ask questions to STAND OUT, you shiny thing!

9 Shiny Questions To Choose From:

1. Why do you love working here?

2. Why is the role vacant?

3. What are the top skills and experience you're looking for in the ideal candidate?

4. If I'm offered this position, what would training look like?

5. What are some potential career paths with the organization?

6. What do you see as the biggest challenge for this role?

7. Do you see any skill gaps in what you're looking for in the ideal candidate and my background?

8. Would there be any reason I wouldn't be invited for a second interview?

9. I see from LinkedIn, you've been with the company for 10 years. What do you love about working for the organization?

You don't have to memorize the questions—have them pre-written and take them with you.

Oh, and don't ask them all. Pick your top 2 or 3 questions. Bring all of your questions, but know there likely won't be time to ask them all. You'll also look prepared with additional questions in case the interviewer answers several on the list.

Remember to do this at the end of every interview...

DO NOT LEAVE UNTIL YOU'VE ASKED THESE FINAL 2 CRITICAL QUESTIONS....

1. What is the timing for the next steps in the interview process?

After the hiring manager outlines the date for the next steps...

2. If I haven't heard from you by that date, may I follow up with you?

If you get a yes, **DO IT!**

I always share with candidates what day they should expect to hear from me. And, I say,
"If you haven't heard from me by that day, please do feel free to follow up."

If you're given that GOLDEN opportunity to follow up. DO IT!

Why?

It gives you a chance to be a stand out,
because most people won't follow up.

You'll be a knock out with clever questions!

You should be feeling confident about your next interview.

I hope you've had an Ah Ha while reading this chapter.

The reason your previous interviews were flat-lining disasters is because your resume wasn't helping you. Your rusty old resume caused you to be a meandering mess in your interview.

Spurting out words, disjointed ideas, and rambling thoughts.

BUT, because you're a smarty pants and you followed the easy 2-step formula on how to write a shiny resume, you now know SUCCINCTLY how to describe your role and key successes.

You can answer KEY critical questions to bring your resume to life with EASE. You should now welcome the opportunity to highlight those two or three pages and ACE your next interview.

Your FEAR about interviews should be gone.
You'll ace the interview and get the Zippy Gig!

Congratulations!

Because you put in the effort to create a SHINY resume – you likely breezed through this chapter.

A FUN reward for you - A bonus chapter on all of the little smoking hot things that give you an edge and keep you on track to get your Zippy Gig!

CHAPTER 10
Acing The Video Interview

Video interviews were once a rarity. Since the pandemic, they are now just part of the regular interview process. And they won't be going away.

If video interviews weren't tough enough – now we have the extra challenges of doing them from home (which can be scary and nerve wracking) ...where all sorts of unexpected things can happen. Unwanted cameo appearances from children, spouses and pets. A delivery person incessantly rings your doorbell. Your house alarm screeches or someone in the kitchen sets the smoke detector off. Or even your beloved Fido barks at someone walking by.

OK, I didn't mean to set your heart racing. Don't worry, you can handle all of these silly life situations should they arise in your next interview.

I snapped this picture minutes before going live on a TV news segment. Yes, that's the backside of my giant cat, Phoebe. I joked with the anchor that my cat was still deciding if she wanted to partake in the interview! Thankfully, she opted to lay in the sun rather than appear on television. She did however, make her international webinar debut a few weeks later. She sat on my lap during the last 15 minutes of my ***Hired!*** presentation.

And, that's when I realized, it's 100% OK when a cat, child or spouse accidentally joins your interview.

In fact, EXPECT it to happen at some point. Just smile. Introduce your "guest" and continue on with the interview. It happens to everyone.

Many funny video interviews have hit the media. Two of my favourites:

The Prime Minister of New Zealand, Jarcinda Ardern, was giving an on-camera Covid update when her toddler made a surprise appearance. Jacinda was a total pro in handling it. In her sweet mum voice, she asked her child to go back to bed and said she'd be there shortly to tuck her in. She then went back to the update. Google it – you'll smile.

There was a USA lawyer who was on a zoom call with a judge. He accidentally put a cat face on instead of his camera. I think I laughed for a few hours after seeing that video. Watch it if you need a pick-me-up before your next interview. You'll get some good endorphins from laughing!

One of the things I've loved about our work from home situations is that we were forced to invite people into our homes. The line between professional and personal has become a bit blurred. We interview from our kitchen table or make-shift office, where strangers can meet our loved ones and people get a glimpse into our "at home" lives. The best part – we've all toned down a notch. We've given each other permission to be human. And, that's been downright lovely.

One of my clients shared one of her "guest" appearances by her 8-year-old son. He appeared out of nowhere with a jar of pickles, asking her urgently to open them. The funny part? He was only wearing orange underwear.

7 Cool Ways To Ace Your Video Interview:

1. **Lighting matters.** And it's also tricky. You look like a ghost if there's too much light. Too little light and you blend into the walls. Neither scenario is good.

   Use your phone to find the best light. Flip the camera so you can see yourself. Walk around your home to see where the best lighting is. The general rule, you should always have light, whether a lamp, ring light or window in front of you.

   A few days before your interview, test the lighting at the same time of day your upcoming interview happens. Natural light helps but it still needs backup.

2. **Webcam woes**. My webcam is in the dumbest spot ever. It's at the very bottom of my laptop screen. If my laptop is sitting on my desk, and the camera is turned on, I get an unflattering "under-the-chin and under-the-boobs" angle. HA. At first, I propped my laptop on a dangerously tall stack of books. That grew old quickly, so I opted for an externally mounted camera, which works perfectly. (There's lots of options for external cameras at a very reasonable cost.)

   It's critical that you do a webcam check an hour before each interview. You've likely moved your laptop around and chances are the "stuff" in the background might have changed too! There's a number of on-line free webcam test tools. Just google, "test my webcam".

3. **What's in your background?** Yes, we're looking while chatting with you. I gave a coaching session to a client before his video interview. I jokingly said, "You might want to make your bed and I can see a few beer bottles on the counter...they should be moved to an "off camera" area!"

   Whatever is in the background, just ensure it looks orderly. And, don't blend in. If your walls are white and you're wearing a white shirt, you get lost on the screen.

4. **Test your microphone.** You want to ensure your audio is clear. Not too loud. Not too quiet. Dial up a friend and have a quick test chat or there's a number of on-line tools as well. Sure, there's usually a test on the video platform, but 2 minutes before going live on your interview isn't a good time to find out your mic isn't working.

   Have a set of headphones ready to plug in as a back up in case your computer audio fails.

5. **Have a back-up device.** If you're doing the interview on your laptop or desktop and they fail, have the platform downloaded on your phone or another device. I learned this one the hard way. Minutes before going live on a morning show, the camera on my laptop failed. I broke a sprint record running to the kitchen to get my iPad. Thank goodness, I had the platform downloaded, but my mistake was not having it within reach.

6. **Attire matters**. Dress both the top and the bottom. If you have to dash out of the room to shut off an alarm or calm a barking dog...the minute you get up, your bottom half is on the screen. If you're wearing a jacket and tie on the top but shorts and flip flops on the bottom...well, everyone gets a chuckle.

   Dress exactly as you would for an in-person interview. For more tips on attire, head over to Chapter 12 – the Dressing Sharp chapter.

7. **Arrival time:** Same as an in-person interview, you don't want to be too early or too late. *I know that's vague – read on.*

   I was scheduled for a video prep with a coaching client. Two hours prior to our scheduled time, I received a notification that "Kleck" had logged into the meeting. "Kleck" wasn't the name of my client, so I assumed the meeting was hacked. I logged into the platform and promptly blocked "Kleck".

Take that you hacker!!

I logged back in a minute before our scheduled time and waited. And, waited. She didn't arrive, which wasn't like her. So, I called her. In a panic she said, "I've been trying to log on, but I've been blocked!". I grinned and said, "You must be Kleck."

Here's what happened. She logged on 2 hours early to test the platform for sound, lighting and such. And, you know the rest of the story!

Here's what we can learn from Kleck:

1. **Use one of the webcam and microphone on-line** tools rather than logging on to the platform.

2. **If you'd like to test the platform,** just know that the meeting organizer will get a notification that you've logged on. If you do log on, log off, otherwise it looks like you're 2 hours early for the interview, which isn't a good look!

3. **Use your own name.**

4. **Log on to the meeting *maximum 5 minutes*** before the session.

5. **Rehearse:** Yes, you need to rehearse everything out loud! If you need a refresh on what to rehearse, dash back to Chapter 10.

6. **Technical stuff:** Restart your computer an hour before the interview. Also, a lesson I learned. I was doing a morning show with a local station in Calgary. I was excited! It was a TV personality who I've watched for years. She's a ton of fun and this was our first interview. I was up early to perfect the hair peaks and I was set! 30 seconds into our interview, the platform failed. Conked out. Done. A computer re-start would have drastically eliminated the possibility of this glitch.

7. **Wifi strength matters.** If you're sharing a connection with others in your home, if possible, have everyone log off, so you've got a stealth-like connection. If you're solo on the Wifi, ensure you turn your phone and other devices to airplane mode.

8. **Non-technical stuff:** Put a sticky note on your office door to remind others in your household that you're on a video interview. If I'm recording webinars or doing a live TV interview, I also put a note on my front door asking any visitors to not ring the doorbell or knock.

Lights! Camera! Action!

CHAPTER 11

Smoking Hot Interview Tips

Pre-Interview Prep Checklist.

You've created an amazing shiny resume.
Check.

You've rehearsed out loud how to answer *"Bring your resume to life for me..."*. Your delivery is soooooooooooooo smooth, it will be music to the interviewer's ears. **Done.**

I Want You To Do These 8 Pre-Interview items:

1. **Check the LinkedIn profile of the person(s) you're interviewing with.** It shows you've done some research on the person. You'll learn if you have contacts in common. Perhaps you've attended the same college or university. Take a look at their head shot – is their attire formal or business casual. (It gives you a hint on what to wear to the interview.)

2. **On attire** – plan out the day before what you want to wear. Ensure your outfit is clean and ready to go.

And, have a back-up plan. Yes, pants split. Zippers get stuck. Hems fall. Heels crack. Be ready with an alternate.

3. **Do a dry run to the interview location.** You need to know where you're going. Where's the closest parking? And where's the next best alternate parking? Be sure to leave time for an extra walk if you have to go with "Plan B" parking.

4. **Bring two copies of your resume with you**. You never know if the hiring manager's printer just went on the fritz. Yes, it's happened to me. It's a whole lot tougher for you if the hiring manager doesn't have a resume to glance at during the interview! Their eyes will be glued to you. And, you don't want that to happen. You'll look like a super star if you come prepared with a copy of your resume for you both.

5. **Print/write out your clever end of interview questions** and tuck in your file folder or portfolio.

6. **Bring a copy of your references.** But DO NOT leave them unless they are asked. Refer back to Chapter 14 on references.

7. **Print a copy of the job posting.** And, bring with you anything interesting from the website. (Press releases, corporate mandate, community involvement, etc.) It shows you're extra prepared and you've done your research.

8. **Double check the interview time.** Nerves can do funny things to your memory. Just to be sure – *double check the time.* If you're logging into a conference bridge or video call, ensure you're on time. I've had a few folks blow their chance out of the gate by calling in late. If it is a phone call, be sure to double check – are you to call the hiring manager or are they calling you? Double check this too!

You've got this! We're on a roll! Let's keep going.

22 Quick (& Easy) Interview Tips To Make A GREAT Impression:

1. **Learn to extend a firm handshake.** No limp fish here. But don't be a bone-crusher either. This was a must in pre-pandemic times. Follow the cue of the hiring manager – if they extend for a handshake, respond. Chances are, they'll just greet you with a big smile.

2. **Leave the java in the car.** Bringing a giant *Timmies* coffee is too casual.

.**Sassy Sheila Note:** Never reach across the table to take the interviewer's resume copy. They've been writing private notes and questions throughout. They aren't meant to be shared.

3. **Listen to the question and answer *that* specific question.** Yes, it happens. Nerves hit and the candidate answers a completely unrelated question. If you hear the same question being asked, it is simply because you missed answering the question we asked. ***We're giving you a second shot.***

4. **Arrive no more than 10 minutes early** for in-person interviews. (Go back to Chapter 10 for arrival time for a video interview.) Arriving earlier than 15 minutes is just poor planning. If you arrive 45-minutes early, it's really poor planning. Find a coffee shop in the building or down the street to burn up some of the extra time. Kudos to you for not being late!

5. **Turn your phone off.** Worse yet, if it rings, don't answer it! Yes, that has happened. A lot.

6. **Body language.** Just like mom said, "Sit up straight." Make eye contact (not to the point of being creepy). Don't cross your arms. No eye rolling. No slouching.

7. **Smile.** Look interested and happy to be in the interview chair.

8. **Have quick access to a pen.** It should be clipped to your folder or portfolio. Not at the bottom of your cavernous purse.

9. **Take off your overcoat and stay awhile.** If you leave your coat and scarf on, it looks like you're about to dash the minute things get tough.

10. **If a business card is given – take it.** It's poor manners to leave it on the table.

11. **Breathe.** Remember - the interviewer wants to find every reason to hire you. Just help them to be right.

12. **Make eye contact.** Smile with your eyes. Yes, try it. It works.

13. **Be excited to be at the interview.** Many a candidate has blown it simply because they projected an air of disinterest. Be interested.

14. **Have energy and enthusiasm in your voice.**

15. **A nice portfolio** or even a file folder will work to hold your documents: resume, references, details about the company, position posting and other documents.

16. **Laptops, tablets or iPads** can work well, as long as they don't take up a huge amount of time to open. I've interviewed many candidates who spent most of their time looking at their screen and they forgot to look up to make eye contact.

17. **If you're in a design profession** and need to show your portfolio, of course you're the exception. (But still have it prepared and ready) For the rest –a paper resume works much better!

18. **If you think, "Gosh, I've been talking for a looooonnnnggg time."** It has been. Stop talking. Re-group. If you feel you've meandered off topic. Say it. Grin.

19. **Always go solo to an interview.** This isn't an event to take children, friends, parent or spouse. (As I write this, a woman brought her husband to her interview. Worse yet, he had a case of the "ah-hems" and a serious nasal issue. I would have left my office to offer a tissue, but I needed to keep writing. She didn't get the job.)

20. **Let your personality shine through!**

21. **When you interview with an agency recruiter it *is an actual interview.*** We hear all of the time, "Oh, I'd never say that in a 'real' interview. I'm just telling *you*." Oh, the stuff I've heard!

22. **There are loads of snazzy words to use to make a point besides swearing.** I still chuckle at the lovely candidate, leaned in with a hushed voice and said, "Could I curse when I tell you this story?" GRIN. While I can't tell you the story, it sure made me laugh!

If you've done your homework in creating a shiny resume with shiny results, you'll exude confidence and be beaming. We've already covered examples of great questions, so you're set!

CHAPTER 12

Dressing SHARP Gives You An Edge

"Style is a way to say who you are without having to speak."

Rachel Zoe

This is a little chapter but BIG on how it can help you get hired.

From the minute you shake hands and say hello to the hiring manager, judgments have already started about your overall image and rightness for the role.

"It only takes 7 seconds for us to judge another person when we first meet them."

Linda Blair
Author of Straight Talking

7 SECONDS

By the time you get to the hiring manager's office the first 7 seconds have already ticked by and the impressions have started.

Let's talk about why being SHARPLY dressed is critical.

Why? It gives you a big competitive edge.

The first 7 seconds are a scan of how you're dressed, cleanliness (clothes, shoes, hair, hands) how you smell, how you shake hands, eye contact and the confidence of the first words spoken.

"After I put on my suit, I thought to myself, "I look so f'ing sharp, I could cut someone"

Urban Dictionary.com

That sentence made me LAUGH!

It might be a bit extreme, but you'll sure remember it when you take a last glance at yourself in the mirror before heading to your next interview.

SHARP means you have it TOGETHER and you look like it in every way.

Ironed, pressed, put together, clean, covered (more on this one a bit later). You've put thought into it.

You know who you are and how you want to express yourself.

So How Can You Be Sharp?

You can be sharp in a business suit.

Sharp in clean jeans and work boots.

Sharp is an attitude.

You're completely put together on the outside and on the inside. Buffed, polished and put together. You're confident and prepared.

Sharp *also* means what your hair, jewelry, shoes, car, phone, purse, bag, nails, laptop, pen, and coffee cup look like. You don't have to spend a mint. You can be budget friendly and still look put together.

"In our industry wearing jeans to an interview is fine, however, ensure that they are clean, not ripped and that you have a decent shirt on – not one from a Metallica concert. Yes, it's a true story."

Sue Wood, HR Advisor

Here's A Stat To Make You Shine Your Shoes:

"95% of interviewers think an applicant's appearance in an interview is a reflection of their professionalism."

Source: Nvision Survey

Dress For The Role You're Interviewing For.

Since I was a little kid, I've always wanted to wear a suit and carry a briefcase.

True story.

I recall seeing a magazine cover with a woman wearing a navy suit and carrying a briefcase. It locked into my 5-year-old brain. That was going to be me. As a 5-year-old I had no idea what my job or my career was going to be.

Copyright © Sheila Musgrove

But I certainly knew what I'd wear!

Dressing well IS dressing SHARP.

If you're interviewing for a corporate position, you should be in a suit. This goes for all genders. If you know the corporate culture is more relaxed, then ditch the tie.

If you're interviewing for a role in an industrial environment – then dress how you would go to work. Still aim for SHARP.

This is a huge opportunity to stand out with your personality and confidence!

I have a bit of an unusual style which is distinctly me. From my crazy-ass hair to the big jewelry – it is all part of my personal brand. Which on the great news side, people tend to remember me!

So, go with your style.

I cringe when I hear antiquated advice such as:

Don't wear bright colours.

Don't wear bright lipstick.

Keep your hair conservative. *(I just burst out laughing.)*

Don't wear statement jewelry.

Wear a low heel.

Don't wear loud socks or tie.

Don't wear crazy stylish shoes.

Toss. It. All. Out. The Window.

If I took any of this advice, you'd never recognize me!

Do you. It's your style and part of your professional brand.

Show a future employer your work style.

Sharp Details Make A Difference. And Make You Sharper.

Remember the last time you bought a car?

You went over that baby with a fine-tooth comb before you bought it.

You checked for every little detail that showed you how this car has been taken care of.

Well. You're a car. Or maybe a half-ton...

Details show that you *pay attention* and you look at the *bigger picture* as well.

- Shoes must be shone. They also can't squeak or have run-down heels.
- Jeans are good in lots of situations. If you apply for a role where jeans are acceptable to wear to work each day, then they're absolutely OK to wear to the interview. Jeans with rips fall in and out of fashion (I have a pair or two myself) however keep those pairs tucked away for non-work events.
- Cleavage is a no-no. Corporate = covered.
- Nails must be clean. The only exception would be a mechanic. If you're using polish, ensure it is free of chips and cracks.
- Shirts should have sleeves – even a short sleeve. Sleeveless is just too casual.
- Flip flops – absolute NO. Unless of course you're interviewing for a job that requires you to wear them every day! If you wear an open toed shoe, your twinkly toes must be in top notch shape, with a recent pedicure. If your heels could double as sandpaper, cover them up too!
- Sunglasses should be tucked away. While a lovely fashion statement to have them on the top of your head....it is too casual for an interview.
- For anyone with short hair – aim for a trim every 3 – 4 weeks to keep locks looking sharp.
- If it is raining take an umbrella. The drowned rat look just doesn't work.

- Purses go on the floor – never on the desk or interview table.

- Careful on the perfume and cologne. Be conservative, if not, skip. Think about hair spray and products, deodorant, body lotion...they all have a scent. The last think you want is for the hiring manager to be sneezing and wheezing if they're scent sensitive.

Sidebar story:

A few years ago, I met a candidate who looked like she'd just walked out of the shower. It was pouring rain out – I'm not sure how far away she parked, but between the water dripping off her hair, and on the floor, along with her soaked clothing, she only had a quarter of my attention! And, that was *after* I suggested she zip to the washroom to dry off before we started the interview.

Key Takeaway: Always bring an umbrella. I'd like to focus on your shiny results vs. the puddles.

A quick story on what NOT to wear.

I was interviewing for our receptionist, (who we call the Director of Awesome). I wanted to find someone who was AWESOME in every way. Attitude, personality, talent and of course an extension of our brand. It takes about 15 seconds to look at our website and figure out what the style of the team at TAG. Sharp, crisp, professional would be a couple of words to describe us. And, everyone is in a suit.

"71% of interviewers will pass on a candidate who isn't appropriately dressed."

Source: Inc.

Sooooo, imagine my surprise when I went to greet my first candidate of the day and GASP, she was wearing a skort *(no, that isn't a typo – a skort is a skirt but with shorts underneath. It is a clever piece of clothing.)* She wore 100% golf attire, right down to her shoes.

I didn't really care that she went golfing early in the morning.

But I did care that she wore the same clothes to our interview. And I wasn't interviewing for a golf pro and even then, it wouldn't have been appropriate.

She failed the first 7 seconds.

When you arrive to an interview, you're showing me the best version of you.

If you come to an interview in golf attire, I can only imagine what you might wear on a casual Friday. Tank top? T-shirt? Yoga pants? Flip flops? GASP.

If you need to change out of work clothes and into interview attire, find a place to change so you're sharply dressed. If Clark Kent can turn into Superman in a phone booth, you can find a place to change into your sharp interview outfit.

Make Your 7 Seconds Count!

"Dressing well is a form of good manners."

Tom Ford

CHAPTER 13
4 RARE Occasions When It's OK To Cancel An Interview.

Oh noooooooooooooooooooooooo.
You've done all this work to finally be invited to the interview. It is set and *now you can't make it.*

You don't know what to do and your heart rate is in the red zone?
Don't worry.

The 4 RARE Occasions You Can Cancel An Interview:

1. You're SICK.

Since the on-set of the pandemic, we've all become hyper-sensitive to anyone with the sniffles or a cough. Stay home. The hiring manager would rather see you at your best and not be worried about being in a room with you. Stay home. Postpone the interview.

We've seen way too many go-getter candidates go to their interview and BLOW it because their energy and enthusiasm are low. And, when we ask what the heck happened in the interview, they say,

"Oh, I didn't feel all that great. I guess I didn't bring my A game."

You're right. If you don't bring it, you don't get the job.

2. Something RATTLED you to the core.

A stellar candidate was about to walk into her first interview with our client. She took a phone call with some terrible news about a family member. She was shaken and devastated. But she walked into the interview with her head in that terrible news and blew it. The interview lasted no more than 20 minutes. And, the door on the gig was firmly closed.

She should have called us to ask that the meeting be rescheduled.

Points for showing up for both of these scenarios – BUT, because they weren't fully in the interview head space, they lost out on the opportunity.

3. You're going to be LATE.

This one could go either way. Being late is usually just poor planning. If there's a major traffic disruption, snow storm or other reason causing a major delay for EVERYONE, then it can be OK.

Call the hiring manager or recruiter. If you're going to be more than 10 minutes late, it is best to reschedule.

If it is just poor planning, you may not get a second chance.

4. Silly things happen.

Loads of silly things can happen. You get in the car and split your pants. Your pen explodes on your white shirt. Your heel breaks off. All sorts of things can happen. I'd rather you cancel than see more of you than I'd like – or see you not at your best. If I took a call from a candidate who had the sense of humour to share a moment – I'd giggle for sure and gladly re-schedule.

Stuff happens...

I'll share one of my "silly moments". This is what my eyebrow looked like after my head came in contact with my front closet door en route to the office one morning. I called my team to say I'd be in as soon as I stopped the bleeding...5 stitches later I arrived at the office.

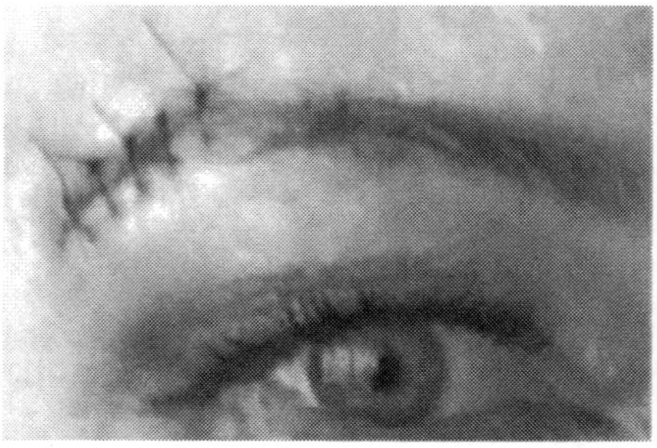

You just have to chuckle when silly human stuff happens. Own it. Find the humour and move on with your day.

"A good laugh makes any interview, or any conversation, so much better."

Barbara Walters

If the STUFF causes you to not be fully present in the interview - be honest, call and reschedule. Most hiring managers appreciate honesty and will likely reschedule.

When it's NOT cool to cancel an interview:

The day of the interview isn't the time to cancel. Unless it's for one of the rare reasons I just mentioned.

If a candidate cancels an interview with me an hour or minutes before the scheduled time, they hit my **#shit** list.

Even if you aren't sure about the GIG, ***GO to the interview***.

1. You might learn more about the role in the interview and realize it is an AMAZING role.

2. The hiring manager might have another role in mind for you that isn't advertised.

3. There might be another connection to the manager for an even better role within another department or company.

4. The role you interviewed for might not be a fit, but the PERFECT role comes up with that manager in the coming months. You'll be on speed dial once it does.

5. You might end up with an hour with a recruiter (like me) who'll give you an hour of intensive resume and interview coaching that's a game changer.

The point is – you just never know what unexpected, fabulous outcomes might arise.

Don't over-analyze. Don't be a chicken. It is an hour of your time. Just GO.

"Sometimes the bravest and most important thing you can do is just show up."

Brene Brown

CHAPTER 14:
References – Powerful Stuff You Need to Know.

This chapter starts with a big bonk on the head.

NEVER offer your references unless requested.

Why?

It's a super awkward moment at the end of the interview. The interviewer hasn't asked for your references; and if you pull them out, slide them across the table and say,

"Sooooooo, would you like my references?"

You've made everything awkward and you don't look professional.

Yup, as awkward as it is for you, it's equally awkward for the interviewer to accept them... when they're not interested. It's kind of like having a bad first date and asking for another when things clearly didn't go well.

Promise me you'll never do that. Even if you feel the interview went great.

Let's face it. Being the candidate and sitting on pins and needles through the whole interview process sucks. You often feel in the dark.

You ask yourself over and over...

Will the hiring manager ever call? Am I still being considered?

(I share a MUST DO at the end of every interview in Chapter 9, which helps you to keep you in the "know" during the interview process.)

If the hiring manager DOES ask for your references, you know you're still in the running for the role.

Know this. A hiring manager will only request references if they're interested in the next step in the interview process.

Who can be a reference?

1. The best reference is someone you've reported to directly. Your boss.

2. Volunteer work – it can be the person you report to.

3. Coaches – if you've been involved in sports during school, a coach can talk about your discipline with training, teamwork & sportsmanship.

4. Teachers or professors – they can speak to your academic qualifications, interactions with classmates and leadership skills.

Details you need to provide when submitting references:

1. First & last name.

2. Title and company they held when you worked together. (This just helps the hiring manager to identify which role on your resume aligns to the reference.)

3. Current title and company.

4. Email and phone number.

Okay. This is a MAJOR step that you can't skip.

You MUST call or email your references to share:

1. Who will be calling them and when.

2. The company name and role you've applied to.

3. If it's been a while since you worked together – give them a bit of refresh on some of the key points you'd like highlighted in the reference call.

And, ask your references to let you know when they've been contacted. The offer is usually presented a few days after the reference calls are completed. If, for whatever reason you haven't heard in a day or two, follow up with the hiring manager to indicate you've heard from your references and ask if there's any additional details required and/or timing of the next (and hopefully, final) step.

It's also a GREAT idea to mention to the hiring manager in your interview that you'll share your references as soon as you've been able to reach them for a "heads up".

You'll be a stand out if you do this. Why?

1. It shows you're taking an extra step to ensure your references are prepared and expecting the call.

2. You make things easier for the hiring manager by advising when your references are available.

Here's an example:

Mary is on vacation for the next two weeks, however, please call on her personal cell at 403-291-2234 between 8AM and 10AM MST this week. She's expecting your call.

3. When you email your references, you can add a note to say, "All of my references have been contacted – they are expecting your call."

It shows you've taken the reference stage seriously AND you've taken an extra step that most candidates don't do.

Frequently Asked Questions About References:

1. Can I use a reference if they're no longer at the company we worked together at?

YES. It doesn't matter if they're in a different company or role. The point is, they can talk about your working relationship.

2. Can I use a reference who is in a different country?

YES. In this case, the hiring manager will often reach the referee by email.

3. **Can I use someone who knows me only on a personal level?**

Unless a hiring manager asks for a personal reference, which is rare, then it's a no.

4. **Do I need to write "References Supplied Upon Request" on my resume?**

   Hard no. Everyone knows references are a final step in the process and you'll have to supply them when asked. No need to add this line.

Two Last Tips On References:

1. **Don't overuse your references.** You want them fresh and excited to be sharing all of your amazing attributes with a future employer. You don't want them to be worn out by the time your dream job comes along.

2. **Don't forget to thank them!** Drop your reference an email (or call) to share if you got the job. Even if you didn't get the job, be sure to thank them for taking the time to give the reference. Thank-you cards are also a thoughtful and professional touch.

CHAPTER 15

Follow Up to be a Stand-Out

"Better to be a nerd than one of the herd!"

Mandy Hale

You know all those manners your parents tried to drill into you?

Keep your elbows off the table.
Don't chew with your mouth open.
Look someone in the eye when you shake their hand.
Always take your plate to the sink.
Stand up straight.
Say please and thank you.
Speak when you enter a room.

Mom Betty always reminded me as a kid to sit and be quiet (and be good) when we were visiting. Oh, and sit up straight too. Mom and I giggled when I refreshed her memory on a story. (P.S. – This is Mom Betty.)

I was about 4 or 5 years old. We were visiting one of my parent's friends. This friend had the hippest house I'd ever seen. White shag carpet, white leather furniture – this place looked like it fell out of a magazine. I sat quietly beside my mom as I listened to the adults chat.

Imagine how freaked out I felt when I was given a giant glass of GRAPE juice.

OMG, was she kidding? I was 5. I spilled stuff. All-the-time.

Chances were if I put my little sandwich grabbers on that glass of purple juice, it would just explode all over the beautiful white shag carpet.

Sooooo, my 5-year-old interpretation of good manners was to just ignore it was even sitting there. To this day, it still makes me laugh. It could have been a disaster! So, a good choice. (Even though I really wanted the grape juice!)

Whether you're 5 or 50 – manners count.

Following Up Properly Is NICE and It Shows You're A Class Act.

Following up after an interview is simply nice etiquette. And good manners are always in style.

My top pick for standing out is to send a *handwritten card*.

Old school? Sure. *Old school sophistication.* It's an easy way to be memorable.

It's almost never done. Be a nerd – send a card.

Thank-you cards stay on our desks at TAG for a very long time. Some of the thank you cards have been displayed for close to a year.

That's a sign of how RARE it is. OK, what should you say in a thank you card?

Dear Sheila,

Thank you so much for your time on Tuesday afternoon. I really enjoyed our conversation and learning more about TAG Recruitment and the role with your firm. I am excited to hear from you on the next steps in the selection process. It was really nice to meet you in person.

Very best,

Mary

This tells me you're trying to be a stand out. I like stand outs.

I would like to see more applicants send thank you notes or thank you emails after an interview. Most applicants don't bother to do it. Sending a thank you note – if done reasonably well – will definitely not hurt your chances at a job. More often, it will improve the impression you left after the interview, making you stand out from your competitors.

Shelley Vandenberg, President
Saskatchewan Blue Cross

A follow up email is also a good choice to follow up. It doesn't have the same stand-out factor as a card, but it works too. The card or email should be written and sent the same day as the interview.

MOST candidates don't follow up AT ALL after the first interview.

As noted in Chapter 9 you should always find out the timeframe for next steps at the end of the interview. Once that timeframe has passed, it's absolutely OK to follow up with a phone call or follow up email.

"An opportunity is missed by most people because it is dressed in overalls and looks like work."

Thomas A. Edison

I always invite candidates to follow up with me**. Most don't.**

Why? **It takes some effort.**

You'll have to make note of the agreed follow up date and *actually follow up* with a phone call or email.

For some it feels too pushy.

You might be thinking, "Well, if they were interested in me, they'd follow up with me."

Not always true. The hiring manager can simply be snowed under with other priorities. The recruiter might be off with another more pressing priority. Lots of things can take a hiring decision or timeline off course.

Follow up shows your initiative – it isn't pushy, unless you *turn into a stalker*. (More on how-not-to-be-a-stalker in the next few pages.)

At every stage of the interview process, you're showing an employer how you'd perform as an employee. If you don't follow up, you're telling me that you'll likely not follow up properly in your daily routine if hired.

And, that's not good.

You want to use following up as a GREAT opportunity to stand out with your communication style and to show consistency.

It also gives you the chance to show your *resilience* in handling the comment:

"...thanks for following up, I don't have an answer for you yet".

This isn't the time for showing any attitude. Sure, you might be annoyed that the process is taking longer than expected. *(And, you need to be working because the bills are piling up.)*

It's the time to be gracious, understanding and conversational. Ask when it would be appropriate to follow up again. That'll get you top marks.

"Life is short, but there is always time for courtesy."

Ralph Waldo Emerson

5 Things To Do When Following Up Via Phone:

1. Use your first ***and last name***. *(I'm shocked at the number of professional candidates who don't use their last name. It's a must.)*
2. Remind the hiring manager when you met and the role you're interviewing for.
3. Indicate you're checking in on both the status of the role and timing of next steps.
4. Be **positive** in your tone. If the role has been delayed, simply ask when you should follow up again.
5. Thank the hiring manager for taking your call (or returning your call if leaving a message).

#1 above might seem silly. Wait till you hear this story!

It Was The Multiple Mike Show!

I interviewed 5 candidates on one day ALL with the first name of Mike.

Imagine when I got a series of voice mails from the various Mikes all following up on their interview and status, using only the name, **"Mike".** GRIN. Mike who?

So please share your last name too!

Caution: Avoid Stalking the Interviewer

I worked with a candidate who called me one morning 9 times.

Yes, 9! I was on a long conference call and counted the number of times his call came in.

He went from a strong candidate, to a little bit of a *crazy one*. Thank goodness he was coachable and learned the value of leaving a concise voice mail message, rather than keeping me on speed dial.

"It takes 24 hours to 2 weeks to hear from the company with their decision."

Jacquelyn Smith, Forbes

We'd all love hiring decisions to be made faster. If there are delays, use your conversations or voice mails as a way to continue to make a great impression. The undertone of what you're sharing with your future company is valuable.

You're demonstrating 5 things that can keep you in the running:

1. You have consistent follow up and you call/email when asked.

2. Your professionalism and communication skills are consistent.

3. You can roll with the punches. You understand delays happen.

4. You're standing out amongst others vying for the same role.

5. You're developing a further relationship with the Hiring Manager.

Keep consistent with your follow up and you WILL stand out.

***But don't call 9 times in 1 day. Just say NO to 9.**

CHAPTER 16
You've Got The GIG. Now Negotiate.

Yaaaay! They like you. They want you. Now it's time to **talk salary**.

This can be a scary part. You don't want to go too high. Nor do you want to take an offer that's too low.

In the old days it was a *silly dance*.

Candidates would always say,

"Make me an offer based on my experience."

Bad idea!

Know your value and know the role you've applied for.

You don't need to guess.

I ask candidates 2 simple questions on salary:

1. **Tell me where your compensation is now.**
2. **Where would you ideally like to be in your next role?**

(And, I'll also tell you if you're too low or too high in your expectations.)

(There are some countries where questioning current compensation in a no-no. If so, you'll want to focus on the industry standard of compensation for your role.)

If you're honest with these 2 questions, you're on your way to helping a future employer make a reasonable offer.

Yes, it's normal to look for an increase when moving to another role. You're not jumping ship to just get a longer lunch break.

10 Big Factors To Consider For Compensation:

1. **Base annual salary.**
   - **a.** What is the base salary in comparison to where you are now?
   - **b.** When is salary reviewed? After 6 months? Annually? What are the average annual increases?

2. **Benefits package:**
   - a. Is it fully or partially paid by the company?
   - b. What's covered?
   - c. When does it start? Is it right away or after a waiting period?

   NOTE: *Don't add the value of your benefits package to your salary. It just muddies the water. Keep salary and benefits separate.*

3. **Bonus structure:**
   - a. Is there one in place?
   - b. How is it earned?
   - c. When is it paid? (Monthly, quarterly, annually)
   - d. What % has been paid in the past?
   - e. Is it achievable? How often has it been achieved by employees?

4. **Vacation:**
   - a. How many weeks annually?
   - b. How is vacation earned? (Example: If vacation is 3 weeks annually, ask if it's earned at 1.25 days per full month worked or do you have to work a full year before vacation is taken.).
   - c. Are you entitled to take it in the first year?
   - d. When does the number of weeks increase?

   This can often be a negotiation point to enhance the overall offer. If an employer can't budge on salary, perhaps there's room for extra vacation.

5. **Personal days or sick days?**
   - a. Are they offered?
   - b. How many?
   - c. Is there a waiting period?

6. **Allowances:**
   - a. Cell
   - b. Car
   - c. Mileage reimbursement

d. Travel expenses (per diem)
e. Parking

7. Tools To Do The Job:

a. Laptop
b. Printer
c. Cell

8. Training and Professional Development:

a. Tuition reimbursement
b. Paid membership in your professional association
c. Professional Development courses
d. Industry conferences
e. Networking events

9. Pension & investments:

a. RRSP matching
b. Stock purchase or matching

10. Fun stuff:

a. This is a fun one at my company. You'll get a nice gift certificate and team lunch on your birthday.
b. How are milestones celebrated? At TAG this is a big one. When we hit financial thresholds, we hop in a cab and zip downtown for a lingering lunch at our favourite hot spot. And, one milestone was celebrated with Betty's buns. Yes, my mom (and dad) arrived with pans of her famous buns for lunch!
c. Is there extra time off for the holidays?
d. Do you receive the Civic Holidays in addition to the Statutory Holidays?
e. Gym memberships or other perks?

11. Other stuff:

a. What is the start/end time? Is it flexible?
b. Is it a 37.5 or 40-hour work week?
c. Will you have a shorter commute to and from work?
d. Work environment? Private office? Cubicle?
e. What is the work from home policy?

See the Remote Work Chapter 17 for further reference.

The Hiring Manager Has Made An Appointment To Call You With An Offer—*Here's What To Expect.*

Panic just set in. What do you do? *How do you handle that call*?

Just breathe. A verbal offer is a very standard practice. The hiring manager wants to personally walk you through the offer before sending it to you in writing.

Have a pen and paper ready to write notes on the details of the offer.

They will review all of the key elements of the offer. You may want to have a list of questions from the previous page ready. Chances are they'll review every detail of the offer...because they want you to accept it!

You don't have to accept the role on the call. They'll send the offer and give you a few days to think. If they don't say when they'd like an answer, it's a good question to ask.

End the call with a big thank you! And, let them know you're excited to review the written offer.

So Now You Have An Offer But It Feels A Little Light/Wishy-Washy?

They like you. They want you. And now they've offered you something that just doesn't work for you.

You don't want to offend them but you know you can't accept it either.

2 Safe Questions To Ask BEFORE You Sweat Through A Negotiation:

1. **Is the offer firm?**

2. **Do we have any room to move?**

Keep to the facts.

Example:

I'm currently at a total income of XX with base and bonus with XX weeks of vacation. To make a move, I do need to be at XX.

And don't apologize for it.
Don't make excuses.
Don't fumble and flop around.

Make your statement with confidence.

"Unless you know what you want, you can't ask for it."

Jeanne Segal, PH.D

2 Negotiation No-No's:

1. You've given your number on where you'd like to be.... and then you change your mind and drastically increase what you'd like for annual salary. This usually kills a negotiation.

2. Opening up the negotiating conversation after you've signed the offer. The deal is done when you sign.

P.S. It's OK to decline an offer if the numbers don't work. Treat it in the same manner as resigning. By doing it in a professional manner, and declining an offer with class - it will always make you memorable.

Send them a thank-you card.

Your mother would be happy if you did that.

CHAPTER 17

Remote Work Is Here To Stay. But, Is It For You?

In pre-pandemic times, most of us thought it would be AMAZING to work from home. With zero interruptions, we could sail through our work day at stealth-like speed, knocking every "to do" out of the park. And, of course, the house would be spotless. Laundry always done. Not a crumb on the counter. HA.

Working from home for months and years on end????
No way, that's NEVER going to happen.

Pre-pandemic it was a rare for employees to work from home, unless they were self-employed or freelancing.

Employers resisted employees working from home, BIG TIME! While no one said it, employers thought their employees would bake cookies every afternoon and catch a few talk shows in between emails. Productivity would be lost. No way working from home would ever be a "thing".

And thennnnnnnnnnnnnnn...
The pandemic came in like a tsunami.
The world went into lockdown.
Overnight everything changed.
We were all forced into working from home.
Ready or not, that was the only choice, unless you were a front-line worker.

We were in disbelief it was happening. It was scary. We felt like we were hit by a train.

We had to figure out how to mesh our personal lives and surroundings into our professional lives.

Zoom and Teams became household words. Our colleagues met our spouses, kids and pets online. We had a glimpse into what everyone's home office, kitchen table...wherever and whatever our "new workspace" looked like.

It was weird in the beginning. It was a massive shift. We'd never experienced anything like this in our lives. But we adjusted. Because we had to.

A weird new phrase became a buzzword, "***the new normal***". Blah.

What's normal anyway? Life doesn't stand still. It's constantly changing. This shift just happened to smack us all on the head. But secretly, everyone wanted our old normal back.

"Those who suffer the most, are those who resist the most."

Buddhist expression

Confession. I resisted the "new normal." You might have felt that way too.

I thought we'd be remote for a few weeks. A month at the most. HA. Was I wrong.

I'll be honest. I miss my beautiful, contemporary office. The coffee was always on and the play list was unexpected. Everything from AC/DC to Flo Rida and Calvin Harris. It had a cool vibe. A disco ball in the kitchen to help bust a move while the coffee brewed. A giant gong was hit for every success. It was cool and part of the TAG brand.

After a year of not needing to go into the office, except to get the mail and adjust the heat, it made sense that I sell it. I was initially sad. And then I chose to accept versus resist.
My recruitment firm opened a new chapter and everyone adapted really well to

working remotely and we're not going back to an office environment. (Me included!)

Who knew a pandemic would increase our productivity? But it did. If job orders hit before 7AM, we roll out of bed and start working. No need to buff and polish and drive to the office. It's been a huge benefit.

If a day isn't off-the-charts busy, I can carve out some time to work on writing or special projects. I could never write while in the office, as there were too many distractions. Now I say to my team, *"I'm unplugging for an hour to work on a project."* It's been a huge plus for me.

Perhaps down the road, we'll do a hybrid model. *Till then, I'm happy to have a 27 step walk to my home office....in flip flops.*

"77% of respondents said flexibility regarding work location and hours would influence whether they stayed in a job."

Angus Reid, October 2021

If your line of work opts for a work from home situation, here's 7 things to consider to know if it's right for you. If this list freaks you out, then easy-peasy, opt for the type of work that can't be done from home, or search for companies that allow an in-office model.

Work From Home Considerations— BEFORE You Apply For Remote Work:

1. **Where is your workspace going to be?** Many people don't have the luxury of a dedicated office space. You might have to be OK in setting up and taking down daily if your workspace is the kitchen table. You'll need space to tuck away your work items so they can quickly be set up each morning.

If there are multiple people in the space, where can you all work quietly and productively?

2. **Ergonomics.** We all spend most of our day time on our computer. I can tell you first-hand that arm/wrist injuries from too much typing time on a small keyboard are painful. Proper screen height, keyboard and mouse position all matter to help keep you injury free.

Think about where you'll place your laptop, monitor(s), keyboard, mouse and printer. You'll need a good chair too. While it might seem like a super idea to lounge on the couch while balancing your laptop on your stomach - you'll likely end up having an accidental nap or roll off the couch at the end of the day with a sore back. Neither are good!

Things to consider to help with ergonomics: A larger monitor, ergonomic keyboard, mouse position, and seating.

3. **Wifi strength.** WOW – this is critical. If there are multiple people in your living space, with multiple devices, your wifi will freeze. No one can be productive without strong wifi. If so, a booster through your internet provider is an easy fix.

During critical video meetings or interviews, have everyone turn off any unnecessary devices to give more bandwidth. It's probably a good idea to set up some household "rules" on wifi.

4. **Camera.** (See Chapter 10 on camera tips.) For your day-to-day work, you'll be on video meetings daily, if not weekly. You need to consider what your background is or choose a background filter. There's lots of options on the various video platforms.

5. **Lighting.** You need good lighting to work on your laptop and to be seen while on camera. We all need as much vitamin D from the sunshine. If you can work near a window where you'll have natural light, all the better. If not, be sure you carve out some time each day to get outside.

6. **Focus and self-discipline**. Can you leave the TV off during the day and keep your social media time to a minimum? You need loads of self-motivation. Can you work alone and only have contact via phone or video? Or do you need in-person energy?

"More than 90% of employers are planning to adopt a hybrid working model for their knowledge workers in 2022."

Harvard Business Review

7. **Multi-person household.** You have to consider noise levels and overall household activity. How will you concentrate? If you're the only person working from home with a stay-at-home spouse and children or a roommate – you'll need a cue to indicate you're working. Maybe it's a closed door with a note or if you've got your headphones on, it's a signal that you're "at work" and can't be disturbed.

It should be pretty clear after reading this list, if a work from home situation is right for you. If it's not, there's loads of careers that can't be done remotely. The work location will always be shared in the job posting.

"29% of Canadians worked from home from July 2020 to June 2021."

Source: Government of Canada. 2021 Labour Force Survey

Benefits of working from home (WFH):

What did Dorothy say from *The Wizard of Oz*?
"There's no place like home!"

1. **No commute time**, giving you extra time for outside work interests and family.

2. **Cost savings:** dry cleaning, transportation, dining out, business attire expenses.

3. **Work/life balance**. During your lunch break, you can take a quick stroll around the block, put on a load of laundry or peel potatoes for dinner.

    A good friend decided to paint her garage door on her lunch breaks. That's something you can only do in a WFH situation!

4. **Less interruptions.** Higher ability to concentrate.

5. **Comfy clothes and shoes.**

6. **Relocation to a more cost-effective community.** This may be a great time to relocate to a smaller community or closer to family.

7. **Work from an exotic location**. If you live in a cold climate like I do, your employer may allow you to leave the country or province in your WFH situation.

"46% of remote workers are planning to move to a new location this year because they can now work remotely."

Work Trend Index – Microsoft.

8. **If you're in a smaller centre,** you can now apply on jobs in major centres. Your job prospects will look vastly different now.

Interviews & Working From Home:

Get ready to share the details about your work from home situation and ability in an interview. If you're doing a video interview, the hiring manager will already have insight into your workspace.

Be prepared to share your workspace plan. Use the above checklist to guide the conversation. It shows you're thorough and have the proper resources and processes to do remote work.

Ask Potential Employers:

1. What office supplies are covered or expensed?

2. Are laptops, monitors and printers provided?

3. What is your WFH policy? Is it blended? Is it optional?

4. What is your policy on location? Some employers have policies on the number of driving hours you need to be away from the head office.

5. Is there a set start and end time for each day or is the workday flexible?

6. Clarify if you'll need to keep an eye on email or texts during off hours. Most employers encourage you to "turn off" for the evening and weekend so you can re-charge.

Ask these questions when you're in the final stages or when you're discussing the offer.

And let's not forget about our furry family members. They need to adjust to having you at home and may want to assist with your work.

This is my beloved Phoebe. She gets overtime pay.

She was lucky to have had her paws manicured right before the pandemic and lockdown hit!

CHAPTER 18
How to Resign Like A Pro

Rules for Breaking Up.

I know, I know.

Breaking up is so hard to do in both personal and professional relationships.

You want it to be a break up not a blow-up. No dynamite.

Listen.

You made the decision to look for a new position and thought *that* was the tough part.

But there's one more step.

For many people, the hardest part of making the move to a new job is the resignation. Break ups are never easy. (Especially if you like the people you work with.)

Some of course dream of telling their former boss some precise reasons for leaving, and many dwell on how wonderful it might be. GRIN.

But this isn't the time for you to be aggressive or tell your boss where to go.

Resign with grace. Always.

Work hard and keep focused during your notice period. You'll very likely someday need a reference from your manager. Being respectful, hardworking and professional right to the end of your last day keeps you in the good books.

Think about ways you'd *never* want to be dumped personally. The same rules apply in breaking up with your company.

Ways *not* to break up

(as pictured – *don't do this!)*

- Text message
- Sticky note
- Voice mail
- Email

Don't let technology make you a coward with your boss either.

Think about the **TIMING** - you'd never want to be dumped on a Friday night. OK, well maybe it would be a good thing as you'd have your weekend free!

When is the best time to do the deed?

Resignations are best done on a **Monday morning**.

Your manager then has the full week ahead to get their plan in place on how to allocate your work, cross train and find your replacement.

And, the **LOCATION** – you'd probably want to be in private, not in the middle of a theatre performance or in a restaurant if you were dumping or being dumped personally.

Resignations are best in your manager's office or board room for a private conversation.

Over twenty years I've had my fair share of employee BREAK UPS. Most were done professionally.

I have a few FUN stories to share of what NOT to do.

1. The Drift Off Into The Sunset Approach

One of my recruiters knew he wasn't making the grade and it was obvious I was going to schedule THE conversation soon. He left that afternoon, said goodbye and the usual, *"See you tomorrow"*.

I walked by his office a short time later to find his office key left on his desk, personal items removed and I never heard from him again.

2. The Down To The HOUR Resignation

Another funny one *(in retrospect*) was a recruiter who calculated what she thought she was owed for sick days, vacation and all sorts of other weird things – *right to the hour.*

She resigned on a Wednesday at 1 PM and calculated her notice down to the hour. Yes, she was leaving on Friday of that week at 11 AM. That one still makes me giggle.

3. The "I'm Giving You NOTICE That I'll Be RESIGNING" Notice

I received a text at 7AM on a Monday morning saying, "*We really need to talk today.*"

Just as in a personal relationship, the phrase:

We really need to TALK is code for "*we're breaking up*."

He Was Classy Right To The End.

The best resignation comment I've ever received? After receiving his letter and having the brief conversation, my recruiter said....

"Can I have a hug? *I really don't want to be in your next book on how to not to resign." GRIN.*

(*Mark, I always told you that comment was sooooooooo going in my next book.*)

5 Rules for Breaking up Professionally:

1. Letter of Resignation: We're done.

It should be professional, positive and include the notice period being provided and the date of your last day being worked.

Being gracious is always in style. Thank your company for the time, learning, support and opportunity they've provided you. It will be appreciated.

Keep It Professional & Brief. You're Not Writing A Soap Opera Here.

It should be on a blank piece of white paper **– *NEVER on company letterhead.*** Your message is from you, not a message from the company.

Sign the letter. Place it in a blank white letter sized envelope.

Example Resignation:

Dear Stella,

Please accept this letter as my formal resignation from ABC company. My last working day will be (insert date).

I am very grateful for the extensive professional development and support you've given me over the past 5 years. I have appreciated your support, mentoring and guidance in shaping my career.

Very best,
Bob Smith

2. Notice period:

Personal break ups are best handled like ripping off a band-aid. We're done. Just done. Over. Finito. No notice required.

Professional break ups DO have notice periods based on the amount of time you've been with the company. *(If you signed an employment agreement, you may have agreed to a longer notice period. Check your contract before resigning.)*

Less than 1 year: 1 week working notice. Greater than 1 year: 2 weeks working notice.

(The above notice periods apply in Canada. Check your local legislation.)

Loads of candidates feel they'll leave their employer in a huge lurch if only 2 weeks is given. **Not so.**

Where's your head and heart after you've given your notice? It is with your new company.

It becomes difficult, even for the most discerning professional to keep their focus and output at a high level for more than 2 weeks.

If you have vacation owing, it will be paid out. Don't be sneaky and try to use sick pay and vacation time as part of your notice.

The notice period should be working time.

Notice is also intended to give your manager time to reassign duties to the team, do cross training and hire a replacement. This takes time.

3. Mum's the word: Repeat. ZIP thy LIPS.

The first person you tell is your manager.

After the conversation, a formal announcement is made by the company.

As we'll review in the next chapter on counter-offers – you might be surprised with a solution from your manager. How silly will you look when accepting a counter *after* you shared with everyone that you're resigning?

4. The Resignation Conversation: *We're done.*

Either make an appointment or approach your manager when you know they can give you their undivided attention.

Every manager out there knows when an employee walks in to their office and closes the door behind them with an envelope in hand – it's a RESIGNATION conversation.

Chances are you won't even have to say, "I'm leaving."

Expect QUESTIONS.

Where are you going?

What is the role?

Can you share with me why you chose to move on?

Would you leave this confidentially between us for a day or so to let me come back to you with some ideas?

5. Don't Burn The Damn Bridge.

Resign with grace and professionalism. You may not love your job anymore, but do remember the company took a chance when you were hired. They've invested in you with formal and informal training. You've likely expanded your skills which will fuel your career growth.

Don't burn the damn bridge when resigning. You may need your former employer to provide a reference in the future.

6. Spill the beans:

Do share where you're going. If you're headed to a competitor, your employer may choose to have you depart immediately. Handle it graciously.

If it is not a competitor – expect to work out your notice.

Leaving on positive terms is how you want to leave your organization – the world is small, and getting smaller each day, so one just never knows what paths might cross again!

And you'll always be remembered for being the class act you are.

CHAPTER 19
The Counter Offer – Let's Not Break Up

You've invested a lot of time into finding a new *Zippy Gig*.

You're probably feeling pretty good about yourself and it shows.

You've been through a lot to get to this point:

- Resume writing.
- Countless hours of searching for your *zippy new gig*.
- Preparing for and going through the first, second, third interviews.
- Reaching out and prepping your references.
- You've bitten your nails waiting on interview feedback

And then a JOB OFFER is extended.

YAHOOOOOOO!

You're excited, scared, nervous and happy. It feels RIGHT. It's time to make a move.

You've carefully planned your RESIGNATION.

The letter has been drafted.

You're in your boss's office (likely with your voice shaking, heart rate up and palms sweaty) – the conversation has taken place, the letter has been handed over...

And then the unexpected happens...a **COUNTER OFFER** is proposed.

They don't want you to go.

Why?

They like you. They really, really like you!

The timing might suck for the company, your manager and the team.

There might be a big project about to hit and they need you.

Maybe you were about to get a promotion.

Whatever the reason, they don't want to break up.

Their counter offer is completely unexpected – and hits you completely off guard.

You decided you wanted a new gig...

Or have you?

In with the old—out with the new? OR In with the new—out with the old??

Old Jeans OR New Jeans??

A New Way To Look At Counter Offers.

You've pulled out the old favorite pair.

You put them on and (GASP) they just didn't fit quite right. Maybe a bit too tight. Perhaps too short. Or too saggy in the ass. They just didn't make you happy. You folded them and put them back in the closet.

You then found yourself at the mall in search for jeans that make you SMILE. We all know when we've found THAT pair of jeans that give you a bit of attitude.

They look good. Feel good. Likely you get a double take or a nod of approval from the sales person.

The jeans are AMAZING. You dash to the cashier to complete your purchase.

Excited, you zip home to try them on again and you start planning how these amazing new jeans will fit into your wardrobe.

And then. You spot your old jeans in your closet.

Two things can happen.

You try those old jeans on and they feel AMAZING - like finding an old friend. They just fit. Maybe you've been working out and they fit perfectly.

OR

They feel old, worn, out of style and don't fit like they used to. And, they don't make you happy. Especially when you compare them to the new pair.

Your old company might be like this old pair of jeans. Either you still fit with your existing company or you don't. Something doesn't feel right which is why you started looking for a new job.

And now with the unexpected counter offer you have a decision to make.

A Counter Offer Can Take Many Forms:

- More money, bonuses, holidays, perks
- A change in work area - from the cubicle by the bathroom to the nice one in the corner with a view
- Remote work options that allow you to work from your kitchen table or from a villa in Mexico
- A position title change
- Additional training to get you ready for a new role
- A mapped-out career plan for future growth
- Formal career mentoring
- Share options

For most, a counter offer is responded to with a ***"Thanks, but no thanks."***

But to some candidates, it may be *very tempting*.

3 Things To Ponder Before You Respond:

1. Remember why you looked for a new job in the first place.

Review your list of the reasons WHY you're seeking a move from your present employer. You need to understand what would keep you in your current job and also *why* you want a new one.

Think back to Chapter 1 – the REASONS why you're seeking a new *zippy gig*:

a. More responsibility.
b. More money.
c. Current environment/conditions stink.
d. More balance with work/home.
e. Not the right role – not a great fit with the people or company.
f. No (or not flexible) remote working options.

2. Does the counter offer fix all of the reasons why you were seeking a move?

Has the core reason you were looking for a new job been addressed?

Is the new job you've just secured worth giving up?

3. Never make the decision on the spot.

If you walk into your manager's office to resign and find yourself in an attractive counter offer situation– do this.

Give Yourself 24 Hours To Think.

Don't feel compelled to make a decision on the spot. Don't be pressured into it either. Take some time to ponder what the counter offer means to you. Go with the one that your intuition tells you is the best. Trust your gut.

"The most radical thing I ever did was to stay put."

Grace Lee Boggs

When Is It OK To Accept A Counter Offer?

1. Your manager offers a solution you didn't even think was a possibility.

I had a long-term employee who came into my office with tears in her eyes as she handed over the dreaded letter.

Cindy's husband had secured a job in another city.

She had to resign as they were moving.

In a split second, I said,

"Well, why don't you just work remotely from the new city?"

We both GRINNED with excitement.

There WAS a solution. She didn't have to resign. We were both thrilled.

Listen to the solution. Give yourself time to think and ponder.

2. Show me THE money.

You love everything about your job.
You LOVE your co-workers, clients, and environment.
You love everything.

But you need to earn more. There's no doubt about it.

If you're in this situation, I STRONGLY suggest you have a conversation with your manager *well before* you start a new job search.

Perhaps there's a pay for performance solution or a change in job duties that could result in higher pay and you being happier.

If money is the only stickler and a solution can be found,
it's a GREAT reason to accept a counter offer.

3. You had a brief hiatus from your former employer.

The gig you went to wasn't what you thought it would be. It was a mistake. You feel it in your gut.

If you resigned professionally, that door might be wide open for you to return to your old job.

If the counter offer feels right, chances are it is. Going back to your former role, OR staying put to accept the counter offer can be a great decision. Only you'll know if staying put or moving on is the right move.

Give yourself time to ponder both options. You should be flattered. You've got two great options to consider.

Lucky you!

CHAPTER 20

Creative Resilience During Your Job Search.

Job searching is tough. Rejection. Uncertainty. It's hard. Looking for a new job is one of the most stressful things you'll go through. It's right up there on top life stressors such as moving, divorce or losing a loved one. I get it.

"On average each corporate job attracts 250 resumes. The typical employer will then interview 4 – 6 candidates for the job, and only one will be successful."

Source: Glassdoor

Yeah, that's a lot of resumes that won't hit the bullseye. Don't worry. That's a worst-case scenario.

Read on. I've got some sunshine sprinkled through this chapter to put a spring back in your step!

"If you're going through hell, keep going."

Winston Churchill

Job searching takes time.

"Average amount of time to find a job is 24 weeks."

Source: Bureau of Labor Statistics, USA.

Ugh. ***That's just shy of 6 months.*** To get through, you need a plan. Searching for a job can feel like a full-time job. It's all-consuming. Don't worry.

I have some creative tools & strategies to make these next few months manageable.

Money Management:

To focus on a strong job search, you need to ensure you've got cash coming in to cover living expenses. This one isn't fun, but it's necessary to look at. Desperation can't be part of your job search.

If you've received a severance, map out on the calendar how long it will last. Are you being given a lump sum – if so, ensure you're budgeting out the funds to last 6 months (or longer). If the severance is monthly, look at your expenses and ensure you're managing within the payment that's coming in.

Are you eligible for government benefits? If so, apply as soon as you qualify as there will be a bit of time between applying and receiving payment.
If your funds are light you may need to look at a "**bridge job**". A bridge job is outside of your career path and necessary to keep money coming in. It may be a type of job you've never considered – retail, and hospitality are two common jobs. I think of these jobs as stepping stones... you don't expect emotional gratification from them but they are powerful tools to get you where you want to go. And, they keep $$ coming in.

Don't overlook registering with temporary staffing firms. They often present some really cool job opportunities, which can also lead to permanent gigs.

I'm a fan of using bridge jobs as a strategy. It shows me that you've set your ego aside and will do what it takes to keep money coming in to your household. You're responsible and a realist. You also know that when cash is coming in, things are certainly less stressful.

Track Your Zippy Gig Progress:

Create a spreadsheet or table in Excel or a Word document – use whatever program you're most comfortable with.

Track: Company name, position title, location, date of application and how your application was sent. (ATS upload or via email). If it was sent via email, note the email address. In the rare instances the hiring manager's name is in the posting, add that to your tracking sheet as well.

Print (and save) a copy of the position description. It's always a good idea to print the job posting. It might not be available when you're invited to the interview. And, you don't want to be going in to an interview with only a vague recollection of what the job is.

"A job seeker should focus on quality and not quantity when applying to jobs. 10 to 15 applications per week is a good target."

Source: ZipJob

Let's do the math – 10 jobs per week X 24 weeks = 240 applications. You'll most certainly secure interviews with that number of job applications.

10 – 15 jobs per week should feel manageable. Don't worry if you're applying on fewer or more. Depending on your job category you may find a significant number of jobs to apply for. Conversely, if you're in a specialized or more senior, executive level, you'll likely apply for fewer roles each week, simply because you're in a smaller niche.

4 Daily Job Searching Must-Do's:

Here's a list of activity you need to do every day: *(Yes, you can take a break on the weekend.)*

1. **Carve out time each day to review job boards**.

   Dedicate time each day to reviewing postings and applying. At the moment, there are two primary job boards in Canada: LinkedIn and Indeed. If you're in the USA or other country, there are other predominant boards.

"Job Seekers will spend on average 11 hours per week looking for work."

Source: CareerBuilder

2. **Research top company lists.**

   Top 100 employers, 50 best companies, etc. Go to the individual company websites to view jobs. Larger companies don't always post to job boards. They may rely on their reputation and brand to drive applicant activity.

3. **Set up alerts:**

   Set up alerts on the types of jobs you want to be alerted to on each job board and LinkedIn. This saves you time each day, with new open jobs being delivered to your inbox.

4. **Engage your network**.

   Reach out to your closest contacts with a phone call or email to let them know you're looking.

"85% of jobs are filled through some sort of referral."

Source: LinkedIn

Review your connections on LinkedIn. You're likely connected to people who you may not have ever met or had direct dealings with. They may be exactly who you want to connect with, *if they are hiring.*

Avoid asking for a "coffee meeting" with everyone in your network. Don't do it. Sure, there will be the former colleagues and managers who would love to get together for coffee and chat for an hour over a latte, but for those a little outside of your immediate network that may be too big of an ask.
In my book ***Unexpected Mentors. Weird & Creative Ideas To Boost Your Career***., I give loads of ideas on how to secure a conversation with a business leader or potential mentor (which could be a hiring manager). I also share why the "pick your brain" coffee meeting is a BAD idea. 😊.

Here's 4 tips to increase your odds of securing a conversation:

1. **Ask for a phone meeting** *(versus in person which is often too big of a time commitment).*

2. **Be specific on what advice or insight you're interested in.**

3. **Ensure the ask isn't too big.** It needs to fit within a brief 5 or 10 -minute phone conversation.

4. **If the phone meeting isn't accepted** – you could ask for the advice via email.

Here are some ideas:

"I'm looking to pivot my career from XX to YY. I see from LinkedIn you've successfully made that transition. Might you have time for a brief 10-minute phone call for a few questions on how you've made that career pivot?"

"Mary Smith suggested I reach out to you. I was part of the downsizing with ACME corporation and I'm active in my job search. She indicated you may be looking to add to your team. Might you have 5 minutes for a brief introductory call? Let me know if you'd like to see my resume first."

"We connected on LinkedIn a few months ago, however we've yet had the chance to have a conversation. I'm active in my job search and see you're hiring. Rather than sending in my resume cold, would you have time for a quick 5-minute phone call?"

If you're new to LinkedIn, *don't worry*—I've got loads of insights on LinkedIn in the next chapter.

Agency Recruiters – How To Get On Their Radar

Here's a secret.

The best way to get on the radar of an agency recruiter is to apply for a job they're working on. If they have an open job and you're qualified for that job, you bet you'll get a call!

Recruiters are paid by the hiring company. The way they make money is by filling their open job orders.

Look for recruiters (or firms) that specialize in your career area. There are specialists for sales, executive level, non-profit, finance, IT, engineering, graphic design, and the list goes on.

Chances are that specialist firm will have at least one open job for you to apply on. If not, you'll likely be able to upload your resume to their website. You could also reach out to one of their recruiters to send your resume directly. Typically, recruiters want to be contacted, so their contact details will be easy to find. Reach out with an email or phone call. If there's a big team of recruiters, check their LinkedIn profiles to see if you have any connections in common and connect from there.

Recruiters with strong niches may still want to meet with you, even if they don't have a role. After meeting, they may do what's called a "skill alert" to one or more of their clients. Simply put, they are alerting your skills to their client with a goal of uncovering a position for you.

Always ask the recruiter to ensure you're made aware of any company that they'll send your resume to. You should always have the opportunity to accept or decline. You don't want them to submit your resume on a job you've already applied on. It looks like poor planning for everyone.

Still No Job Action??

You've sent out a pile of resumes, waited for your phone to ring...and, still no job action?
OK, breathe.

9 Things To Consider:

1. **Is your resume still rusty?**

Are you still holding firm on your old-school resume filled with 2 or 3 pages of bullets? Go back to Chapter 4 to re-look at finding shiny results. That's what *will* make your phone ring. I guarantee it.

2. **Are you applying on roles too far outside of your skills?**

Sure, you may feel ready to launch to the next level in your career, but maybe your skills aren't quite there yet. Consider applying laterally to a similar type of role you most recently held.

"75% of applicants for a given role aren't actually qualified to do it."

Source: Workopolis

Copyright © Sheila Musgrove

It's OK to apply for jobs where it's a bit of a ***small stretch*** on qualifications, but avoid applying for jobs you're simply not qualified for. Hiring managers and recruiters will start to recognize your name if you apply for every job on their board. You don't want to get black-listed by being and "over applier.

3. **Resist being an over-applier.** Don't apply for every job at a company. Yes, recruiters and hiring managers have good memories. If we see an application every morning from you – yes, you might be sent straight to the reject pile.

ATS systems track how many applications you've submitted to a company. Oh. Yes. They. Do.

4. **Consider the state of the employment market.**

If the unemployment rate is high, there's a lot of competition on each opening.

This isn't the time to apply "up", *rather you need to stay lateral or potentially apply "down".*

I worked with a VP level candidate in this type of market a few years ago. He ended up securing a role that he was extremely over-qualified for. The company was over the moon to have his skills in the role. *(They even felt a little guilty to get such an amazing candidate and skill set for the job, but that was the market at the time.)* He was grateful to have a job he enjoyed, even though it wasn't at the level he was previously at. It was a 6-month contract that made them both happy. The market did change and he made a smooth transition back to a VP role.

If you have to take a side-step in your career, know that it's likely temporary.

Conversely, if it is a candidate market *(that's when there's a pile more open jobs and not enough people),* you have your pick of jobs. Companies have to work harder to get new hires in the door. They look at training up and closely look at your transferrable skills. This is a GREAT market to be in when job searching.

5. **Has your type of job disappeared?**

I live in a province that is heavily influenced by oil and gas. A recession hit several years ago, which drastically impacted all careers in this industry. Job seekers had to pivot to different roles and industries. #ohshit

If you're not getting traction on the type of roles you're applying on, is there a similar or closely related job you can easily transition to?

Is your career in demand in a different industry? Can you segue over? Or, do you need to do a complete pivot to a new career? (If so, head over to Chapter 6 to read more about doing a career pivot.)

6. **Reassess.**

Are you applying for the right jobs? Are you qualified for the jobs you're applying for? You might dream of a career in a particular discipline, but look honestly at your skill set and background.

7. **Are you applying at a *weird* time?**

3AM is a weird time to apply. If you email your resume in the middle of the night, it will likely get tossed in with the SPAM mail that arrives during those wee hours. They may miss your application all together.

Think about what message you're conveying to the hiring manager. I always wonder if candidates who apply in the middle of the night will be able to transition to a day job. (The exception is if you're applying on a night shift job, then it's ok! But you still may hit the SPAM file.)

The best time to apply for jobs is during regular business hours.

> **"Employers are most likely to release their job postings by 11:00 a.m. and receive the most applications by 2:00 p.m. The best time to apply for a job is between 11:30 a.m. and 12:00 p.m., so that you can beat the 2:00 p.m. rush."**
>
> Source: Indeed

With these times in mind, it's best to schedule your screen time to be scanning job boards mid-morning to early afternoon.

8. **Are you following up?**

Let's demystify following up. The idea of picking up the phone for most people is scary.

9. **Interview self-evaluation:** Do your interviews still need some work? *If you're getting invited to interviews, but no job offers, chances are your interview skills need some work.*

Here's the do's and don'ts of following up:

1. **Don't follow up immediately after hitting the send button**. I always chuckle when candidates call me 10 seconds after submitting their resume. It might not have even been parsed into my database in those few seconds.

2. **Do wait until you've been through a pre-screen or even better, after you've had an initial video or in person interview.** In Chapter 9 I share the must-do at the end of the interview, which is finding out when next steps will take place and ASKING for permission to follow up on that day. When you've got the green light to follow up? DO IT.

3. **Do follow up with a thank you email or card.** (For wording, dash back to Chapter 15). It shows your interest in the role and makes you stand out.

4. **Don't follow up more than once per week.** You don't want to become an annoyance, nor do you want to look desperate. Always ask when you should follow up next.

5. **Customize the target position for each role.** It needs to be the *exact title of the job you're applying for*.

Think about your last interview(s):

Were there questions you stumbled over?
Did they ask behavioural based questions that you could have answered better?
If so, rehearse stronger answers so you're ready the next time.

What's your tone? I did a phone interview with a candidate last week. I said to him, *"I'm pretty clear on what you don't want and that you're a touch angry at your current employer."* He said, *"Shoot, I didn't think it came across that badly."* **It did.**

Are you rehearsing out loud bringing your resume to life? (Refer back to Chapter 9 on interviewing). Ask a friend to listen to your delivery. Are you talking too much? Too little? Verbalisms?

Is your salary off the mark? With economic downturns and the pandemic, salaries can change. ***Sometimes drastically.*** You'll need to cover this hurdle in an interview. Ensure you're making it clear to the hiring manger that you realize "times have changed". Know the current market value for your skill set. (Google on-line tools to give you the average salary for your city and discipline.)

A final word on resilience…
Key to being resilient is continuing to tweak and adjust: your resume, the types of roles you apply for, your approach, interview skills and follow up.

"Courage doesn't always roar. Sometimes courage is the little voice at the end of the day that says, I'll try again tomorrow."

Mary Anne Radmacher

Ensure you're consistently doing the 4 primary daily tasks.

Analyze the list of jobs you've applied on – tweak when necessary. Re-look at the "**no job action"** list regularly.

After each interview do a self analysis on what went well and what needs work. Make the list as soon as you can after the interview while its fresh. Work on being more prepared for the next interview.

Your next application or interview could be the ONE!

"Fall seven times, stand up eight."

Japanese Proverb

You've got this! Keep going!!

CHAPTER 21

LinkedIn, Social Media & Your Zippy Gig

Copyright © Sheila Musgrove

Yes, *of course* we look.

Everyone looks.

Yet it surprises me how many people think employers and recruiters don't bother to check you out on social media.

If you've made the 11 second cut – you can bet we cruise through your social media platforms at some point through the interview process.

You want to keep your image professional and clean to ensure you get the *zippy gig*.

"Social media doesn't create negativity, it uncovers it."

Seth Godin

New social media platforms for personal use continuously pop up and will continue to do so. Facebook, Instagram, Twitter, Tic Tok and the list goes on.

But you're probably not effectively using the BEST social media platform to get a job.

LinkedIn.

The #1 go-to professional social media site is LinkedIn. It's an extremely powerful job-search tool you need to use.

5 Wickedly Powerful LinkedIn Stats To Get Your Attention:

77 job applications are submitted every second.
200 million+ job applications are submitted every month.
10 million+ members are using the #openforwork picture frame.
45 million+ members are using LinkedIn to search for jobs each week.
4 people are hired every minute.

Source: https://news.linkedin.com/about-us#Statistics

It's a ***critical*** platform for your job search.

8 Quick Points You Need To Know About LinkedIn:

1. **Your resume must match your profile.** Or at least mirror most of it. Nothing sends up a red flag faster than a resume not matching the career history on your profile.

   Recruiters and hiring managers spend a ton of time looking for *passive candidates*.
   That's a candidate who hasn't applied for a job posting (we look at those too!), but often we go digging to find specific skills. We often contact people who may not even have thought of looking for a new job. You never know....it might be your dream job!

2. **The more complete your LinkedIn profile, the better chance you have of being contacted.**

The "about me" section. If you've been looking for work, you might have a headline about the type of job you're looking for. Once you secure your next gig, update this section, *otherwise it looks like you're still hoping for a better offer to come along.*

Just like your resume – *no need to write this section in third person voice.* That's just weird.

"75% of our respondents said staying active on LinkedIn will help you get noticed by recruiters."

Source: LiveCareer 2021

Why do you want to be noticed by recruiters?

We're often working on roles that are not posted anywhere else. We also know our clients well—even if we don't have a current opening, if we feel you're a good fit for a client, we'll do what's called a "skill alert". After we get your permission to share your background with our client, we'll reach out to them to see if they may have a pending opening or if a role can be created.

Once you're in our database, we'll keep updating you on new roles that may be a great fit for you.

Research recruitment firms that work in placing your skill set. It's absolutely OK to reach out to a recruiter with a connection request on LinkedIn.

3. **Browsing Profiles**? There's a tab where you can see who has viewed your profile. It's absolutely OK to look, but just keep in mind, the profile owner will know you've taken a peek. (Yes, if you purchase a premium LinkedIn package, it gives you more options, such as allowing for anonymous browsing.)

4. **Profile photo.** It doesn't have to be a fancy formal professional headshot. You can take your own photo.

A few profile blunders:

You shouldn't be holding any type of cocktail. *Unless that's your job.*

The photo should only be of YOU. The pics with your cat, dog, college pals, spouse, kids or the like, go on Facebook. LinkedIn is all about representing yourself as a professional business person.

Yes, you need a photo. If I see a profile without a photo, I always think, "Hmmm, wonder why?"

The photo should be your business face. No sultry, sexy looks. This isn't the site to get dates. Well, I guess you could, but that shouldn't be the objective.

No sunglasses. Unless you work on a beach.

The photo should look like you. When I meet you, I should be able to recognize you. It should be current.

5. Connections: Start building your network TODAY.

Connect with: colleagues, managers (current and previous companies), former classmates and professors, friends, people you meet at career fairs or networking events.

Hiring managers look at all of your social media. Period. When we look at your professional network, it's a bit of a head-scratcher when a person has 5 connections. Sure, you're going to start there, but it really doesn't take a lot of time to build a network. Work at it regularly. When you meet someone, add them.

As I note in Chapter 11, view the profile of the person you're interviewing with **before** the interview. I don't recommend connecting with them until **after** the interview. When you wait, you can personalize the connection with a "Thank you for the interview" message. (And, pop over to Chapter 15 to learn more about being a stand-out with a thank you card and/or email.)

6. Activity.

Yes, to be noticed, you need to be active – like, comment and/or share posts. Tag people in posts if you think a post relates to someone. You can tag them with the @firstlastname and they'll pop up from your contacts. Then they'll see in their notifications that they've been tagged.

The general rule for posts on LinkedIn is that they're business related. This isn't the place to post your vacation photo album. However, if you snap a photo on your vacation that has a business message, then you're good!

OK, I know what you're thinking.

You're terrified to do a post. What if no one likes it? You know what – it can happen! I have several thousand connections personally and my company page is in the 5 digits. Sometimes a post gets 100 views, other times, 10,000 views. The point is to stay active on the platform to aid in your job search.
Back to posting...I get it. You're putting yourself out there and that's scary. Here's a few ideas to ease into being "out there" on LinkedIn:

Start small. Here's a few easy ideas:

1. Start with liking posts. A click is easy to do.

2. Comment on posts:

"Great share, Linda. I really enjoyed it!"
"Interesting perspective. Thanks for sharing."

See, that's not hard!

3. Congratulate people on new jobs and work anniversaries.

4. Share other people's posts. It's easy and a safe way to get more comfortable with posting. Hit the share button. The original poster is notified their post has been shared. I always like and thank anyone who shares my posts.

5. Follow Hashtags:

Follow specific hashtags that relate to job searching, such as:
#hiring #openforwork #jobsearchtips #interviewtips #resumetips #hiredbook (this is the # I use in most of my posts) #Type of work you're looking for: #techjobs #financejobs #salesjobs #adminjobs #Cityjobs (Use either the city name or airport code – example: #yycjobs #calgaryjobs

6. Add the photo banner - #openforwork

It's an easy way to let your network (*and recruiters who are activity searching for candidates*) know you're open for work.

7. Follow companies:

If you're targeting a specific organization, follow their company profile. It provides insight to the organization that may come into conversation during the interview.

8. Follow high profile business leaders who you admire.

You'll get some top-notch insights from world-class leaders. Liking and sharing those posts are easy ways to be active.

How To Add Connections Like A Pro:

You'll have a much higher acceptance rate on invitations if you personalize with a note. There's a character maximum on the note, so be brief and to the point.

Address what or who you have in common. Maybe it's a volunteer organization or you're both alumni from the same school. **Examples:**

Hi Jason,

You and I both know Mary Jones and Bill Smith. I've worked with them both on XX project. I'd like to add you to my professional network on LinkedIn.

Very best,
Sheila

If you have absolutely nothing in common, but you'd like to connect, put that in your connection request note.

Hi Sheila,

I'm active in my job search and I'm hoping to connect with the top local recruiters. I'd welcome the opportunity to have you in my professional network.

Thank you,
Jake

1000% *what NOT to do* when requesting a connection.

1. **Do not try to sell something.**
2. **Do not try to book an interview or appointment.**

The intention is to make a connection. That's it.

I will always decline an invitation that goes like this:

Hi Sheila,

I represent an off-shore recruitment firm, can I book a 30-minute call with you to share our product?

DELETE.

That's like asking someone to marry you on a first date. LOL. You'd never do it and you'd likely scare the hell out of the other person.

After the connection is accepted, then you're good to start a dialogue. You can use LinkedIn messenger OR look on the connections profile under "contact detail" to see if they have an email listed. Most times it's a personal email – if it is, don't use it.

Follow up after the connection with these small next steps:

1. Send a thank you note for the connection.
2. Indicate your interest in the company and specific role.

Hi Sheila,

Thank you for accepting my connection. I'm delighted to be part of your network. I'm active in my job search and keenly interested in your company. (Insert a brief why). I've forwarded my resume via your career portal for the XX role. I hope to be selected for an interview.

Very best,
Shane

Do not send your resume via LinkedIn messenger, unless requested.

What are hiring managers looking for on your personal social media posts?

A 2021 LiveCareer survey surveyed recruiters and hiring managers:

- **66% of respondents cited looking for red flags as a reason for checking a candidate's social media.**
- **62% of respondents want to get an idea about the candidate and their life.**
- **57% of respondents check if someone would be a good fit for the company culture.**

Recruiters typically look at Facebook and Instagram to gain insight into your personal life and LinkedIn to understand your professional side. Yes, we look.

The basic rule – keep it upbeat and positive.

Ask yourself, *"would a company be excited to hire me after looking at my social media presence?"*

If the answer is no, go back through your posts and delete or hide any that would make a hiring manager (or your mom) cringe.

Hiring is a big investment for a company— estimated at close to 1.5 times your annual salary.

In addition to the interview and references, a quick look at social media is important when the cost of a hire is so high.

So, yes, we look.

And, yes, job offers have been halted because of questionable comments or photos on social media.

Remember – you reveal your personality and values in pretty much everything you do.

And sometimes what may look like an innocent post – has revealed your real intentions.

Sidebar story: We worked with a candidate on a key role for a growing organization. Critical to the hiring manager was having someone she could count on to be with the organization for the next 3 – 5 years. While there was no guarantee of course, they just wanted a strong probability that the successful candidate would stay for the longer term.

Here's what happened.

The interviews were a success. Her references were stellar. An offer was being drafted. And, then....

The hiring manager checked the candidate's previous social media posts. *There it was.* A simple comment stopped the deal in its tracks. The candidate had posted she was thinking about going back to university to pursue an advanced degree in the fall.

BOOM.

Done. The offer was sent to the recycle bin.

As innocent as it was, it cost her the gig. No offer. No further conversation. It was over.

"93% of hiring managers will review a candidate's social media profile before making a decision."

"55% have reconsidered a candidate based on what they find."

Source: Money

Are You Invisible On-Line?

Perhaps you hate social media. Or you're a very private person.

I get it.

BUT in today's world – if you don't have a social media presence, or some form of on-line presence – you're considered invisible.

Invisible means old-school.
Out of date.
Out of touch.

According to a survey from *CareerBuilder* of more than 2000 employees:

35% of employers say they're *less likely* to interview candidates if they're *unable to find information* about them on line.

Job searching IS the time to be visible.

CHAPTER 22

Silly Verbal Isms & Dumb Sh!t People Say.

I had lots of fun and many giggles writing this chapter. Each and every dumb thing written in this chapter has been said to me – *many times*.

If you've poured a glass of wine for this chapter – there's a *spill warning*.

This is a chapter of BLOOPERS I don't want you to make.

These are some silly and over-used expressions to stop using.

1. I have 10 years of experience *under my belt.*

I don't want to think about what's "under your belt".

The belt holds your pants up.
No need to talk about your belt.

2. I bring 5 years of customer service *to the table.*

Bring wine to the table.
Bring potatoes to the table.
Bring dishes to the table.
Bring salads to the table.
Leave the table out of it.

3. I'll return your call at *my earliest convenience.*

You're saying,

"I'll return your damn call, when I have absolutely nothing else to do and only when it's convenient for me. Which, quite honestly, could be never." (SMILE)

Worst voice mail of the day:

Candidate: Hi Mark. Call me back. 403-291-2234.

He left **OUR** office number, not his phone number. Haaaaaaaaaa.

No name and no phone number = No call back.

SASSY Sheila advice warning: ***Things you should know before leaving a voice mail***:

1. Your FIRST and LAST name. We often giggle about this one. You should have no hesitation. No delay. No thinking about it. *Know your name*. GRIN.

Hi, it's Mary? The sentence shouldn't sound like a question OR that you're unsure if that's really your name. Grin.

Hi, it's Mary. Call me back. Ummm, Mary-of-no-last-name. Even if I met you yesterday, leave me your last name.

Hi, it's Mary Robinson. Ahhh, that's all that you have to say. *Confidently* state your first and last name.

2. Your phone number. Know it off the top of your head. Always repeat your phone number at the end of the message. And, leave your number *not my number*. Grin.

3. The position you're calling about. OH, we have lots of funny examples on ***what not to say***:

I'm calling about the job on the computer.

I'm calling about a position you posted last week.

I'm calling about the job on the internet.

I'm calling about the job that I got an email alert on.

4. Rehearse leaving a voice mail message.

Sassy Sassy Sheila advice:

If you're looking for a *Zippy Gig* – <u>always answer the phone with your name. First and last.</u>

"Sheila Musgrove speaking."

If we've set up a phone interview OR you see it's a company calling, you shouldn't ever answer the phone with a meek, *"Hello??"*

At the very least, use your first name when answering the call.

Verbal ISMS To Avoid:

Recruiters listen for a living. We pick up on some verbal isms that can be conversation and interview killers!

- **Ummmm.** Drop the umms – better to say nothing and let your words breathe, rather than stringing your thoughts together with a bunch of umms.

- Would you be the person hiring **"er"**? (Yes, this is an ism – it is a way, albeit a bad way to end a sentence. Rather than asking the question and leaving it at that, there is an attempt at an "or"? but it just comes off as "er". It just sounds dumb.

- **"You know what I mean?"** – Suddenly this has popped up as a way to sum up a conversation. My response is usually, *"No, I don't know what you mean."*

- Overuse of the word, **"like."**

- Ending sentences with **"Right?"**

- **"Things like that...."** (Hint – if you hear yourself uttering this phrase in an interview, know the interviewer wants you to be specific about ***"those things***".) GRIN.

- **"Don't get me wrong**..." Yeah, that's a slippery slope.

- **"Beggars can't be choosers" ...** strike that one too!

- **"Like I said" ...**You're really saying to the interviewer..."Didn't you hear me the first time?"

- **"I don't want to even count..."**

- **"Long story short."** If you say this phrase, chances are the story isn't short. At all.

- "**I've never heard of your company**." Also, not giving you a high star rating if this phrase is used.

Have a friend listen to your speech for verbal isms...we all have something, just make sure it isn't an ISM that gives you a big fat no at the end of the interview!!

Hope you got a chuckle or two from this quick chapter.

We all have days when we say dumb things.

Words come out backward or even jumbled.

You just have to laugh, get back on track and let your shiny, prepared results take centre stage.

"In a survey of over 2000 hiring professionals, 27% said that credentials being equal, they would be more likely to hire the candidate who demonstrated a sense of humour."

Peter Harris, Huffington Post

Let's Recap!

Ditch the Rusty Resume.
Create a Shiny Resume Filled with Results.
Nail the Phone Interview.
Rehearse Out Loud.
Rock Your Interview.
Ask Clever Questions.
Dress Sharp.
Negotiate.
Follow Up.
Get Hired.
Enjoy Your New Zippy Gig.
Copyright © Sheila Musgrove

CHAPTER 23

The End. The Beginning of Your New *Zippy Gig*

You did it!

You've created a shiny resume, delivered a kick-ass interview and you've landed the *Zippy Gig*.

Congratulations!

Drop me a note.

What *Zippy* tips worked? How quickly did you land a job? What improved for you?

Tell me your story**. I'd love to hear from you.**

sheila@hideseekfind.com

Keep in touch – connect with me on Instagram or LinkedIn.

https://www.linkedin.com/in/sheilamusgrove/

https://www.instagram.com/sheilamusgrove_author/

"Everything stinks till it's finished."

Dr. Seuss

Congratulations! *You've done it!!*

I wish you incredible success in your new *Zippy Gig*!

Other Books by Sheila Musgrove:

Unexpected Mentors. Weird & Creative Ideas To Boost Your Career.
2019. Available worldwide on Amazon.

Booking Sheila For A Speaking Engagement & Volume Book Orders

sheila@hideseekfind.com **or visit:** www.sheilamusgrove.com

Connect:

Instagram: @sheilamusgrove_author
LinkedIn: https://www.linkedin.com/in/sheilamusgrove/
Enroll in my blog: www.sheilamusgrove.com

Manufactured by Amazon.ca
Bolton, ON

38177091R00114